INDEPENDENT ACADE

WAVES

Using Restorative Justice with Street Group Violence

Theo Gavrielides

To Jim with great [thanks] for what you do. Theo.

the centre for
restorative justice

Independent Academic Research Studies (IARS)
In partnership with the Centre for Restorative Justice, Simon Fraser University
and the Restorative Justice Research Network

Independent Academic Research Studies (IARS)
PUBLICATIONS
159 Clapham Road, London SW9 0PU, United Kingdom
+44(0) 20 7820 0945, contact@iars.org.uk www.iars.org.uk

IARS is a leading, international think-tank with a charitable mission
to give everyone a chance to forge a safer, fairer and more inclusive society.
IARS achieves its mission by producing evidence-based solutions to current social
problems, sharing best practice and by supporting young people to shape decision
making. IARS is an international expert in restorative justice, human rights and
inclusion, criminal justice, citizenship and user-led research.
IARS' vision is a society where everyone is given a choice to actively
participate in social problem solving. The organisation is known for its robust,
independent evidence-based approach to solving current social problems, and
is considered to be a pioneer in user-involvement and the application of
user-led research methods

British Library Cataloguing in Publication Data
Design by dennis@kavitagraphics, printed in the UK by Russell Press

ISBN **978-1-907641-10-7**

Table of Contents

Tables and Chart

Credits

The title of this book is credited to Ben Lyon, IARS Restorative Justice Coordinator.

Cover Photograph and Page 8: Peace wall at Manchester Arndale Centre, 2011 riots. United Kingdom. By Yohan euan o4 (Own work), CC-BY-SA-3.0, via Wikimedia Commons

Page 18: Riots in Vancouver 2011. Canada. By Andy L (DSC_0466 Uploaded by Skeezix1000) [CC-BY-SA-2.0], via Wikimedia Commons

Page 24: Alexandras Avenue, Athens riots December 2008. Greece. By arpakola at gmail [CC-BY-SA-3.0], via Wikimedia Commons

Page 42: London Riots, Clapham Junction. United Kingdom. By GeorgeRexTA [at gmail [dot] com] [CC-BY-SA-2.0], via Wikimedia Commons

Page 62: Riot Cleanup Heroes at Work in Hackney. United Kingdom. By Alastair [CC-BY-SA-2.0], via Wikimedia Commons

Preface & Acknowledgements:
Professor Dr. Theo Gavrielides

The criminal justice system is continuously challenged with new forms of violence. The world economic crisis is also making governments uneasy about the rising costs of prosecution, investigation and imprisonment. The increasing phenomenon of street group violence (e.g., riots) provided the impetus for this book.

Various promises have been made about the potential of restorative justice in relieving the overstretched criminal justice agencies. These promises have been confronted with strong opposition and claims that restorative justice can do more harm than good. Any researcher should be able to take a step back and look at all hypotheses available. The focus of this book is the potential of restorative justice with group violence that occurs on the streets, and is unilateral, time-bound and non-governmental. The example of riots was used.

The very concept of *group* violence takes away *individual* responsibility. One practitioner told me, "I have been involved in most of the serious UK riots from the late 60s ... the one striking factor I have noticed is that there is a moment when the crowd, often individually violent and threatening, changes to a riotous mob with an almost concerted joint action and a loss of individual choice or control".

We know that restorative justice can render positive results when applied within the context of *interpersonal crime* independently of the seriousness of the offence and the age of the harm-doer. What we do not know is whether the restorative justice paradigm and practices have any potential with *group* offenders who engage in harm doing under circumstances that take away *individual* responsibility.

How is restorative justice possible with these cases, if its ethos and success rely on individual responsibility taking? If the core restorative justice values of empowerment, dialogue, responsibility-taking, compassion, voluntariness, honesty, fairness and dignity are to be respected, then how can these be communicated to and applied with large groups of offenders and victims? How can equity and fairness for the individual be extended to the community? How can groups of rioters come together and collectively enter into a restorative process and outcome? Are there any examples of such restorative practices? Are there any benefits to be gained for group victims and the community, and how can rioters' honesty and commitment be monitored and supported?

These are some of the questions that we set off to answer. In carrying out this research, I was confronted with an impressive rhetoric about the benefits of restorative justice with riots. The truth is that actual cases with riots were hard to find. This does not mean that restorative justice may not have the potential to address forms of street group violence. In fact, this book suggests that the limited number of riot cases that have been tested with restorative practices has been promising. Our analysis of the street group violence phenomenon suggests that its nature presents restorative justice with a unique opportunity to show its potential. One of the key reasons that led us to this conclusion relates to the significant number of rioters who wake up the next day feeling ashamed of what they did. This feeling is rather prominent amongst group offenders due to the dynamics and reasons that encourage mob mentality that leads to harm. As one rioter put it: "I was watching myself doing things I would never do ... The next morning was the worst day of my life. I will never forget the shame I felt ... I still don't know why I joined the crowd".

With the danger of repeating myself and alienating my readers, I will emphasise once again what I have proved in previous publications. As a community born ethos and practice, restorative justice must be developed from the bottom up. Top down structures and well-intended attempts to mainstream it without the community, will fail. Ignore this warning and even more money will be wasted while running the risk of re-victimising affected communities and traumatising offenders.

Aligned with IARS' strapline "Community-led solutions for a fairer society", this book also identifies an additional role for communities. This relates to user-led, evidence based policy that allows the development of criminal justice practices that are grounded in the realities of those they aim to serve. Also in line with IARS' international interest, this book is not about one country. In fact four different countries were used as case studies for conclusions that should be of interest to anyone working in the criminal justice and justice fields.

I will conclude by calling all those working in the restorative justice movement to keep an open mind for the development of new restorative practices. The strength of restorative justice lies in its malleability and innovation. This book argues that new phenomena of violence, such as riots, demand new methods of restoration. This book proposes a model that is not one that restorative justice purists would easily swallow. I call it "Waves of healing" and it focuses on the development of the right infrastructure for restorative practitioners rather than the investment into a single project, method or organisation.

I want to thank all the research participants for their time and trust. Without their honest testimonies, the arguments developed in this report would be a

2

repetition of extant theories and promises. I am particularly thankful to Ben Lyon with whom I have had the pleasure of working for over 10 years. As a leading restorative justice practitioner, Ben has opened my eyes to the realities of the real world. I am also grateful to Professor Mark Winston and the Centre for Dialogue at Simon Fraser University for inviting me to Vancouver as the honoured guest of the 2012 Bruce and Lis Welch Community Dialogue. Many thanks also go to Professor Brenda Morrison and the Centre for Restorative Justice at Simon Fraser University for their friendship and partnership in the larger programme within which this book is placed. I am grateful to Professor Vasso Artinopoulou for her support and advice, and thankful to my new friend and colleague Evelyn Zellerer whose work with restorative circles and indeed her feedback on this book helped me improve my view of the world and how I deal with my own interpersonal conflicts.

July 2012

Theo Gavrielides

Foreword: Professor Brenda Morrison, Director of the Centre for Restorative Justice, Simon Fraser University

Riots: How do we make sense of them? How do we respond to them? Our answer to the first question sets the stage for the second. Different questions set the stage for different outcomes.

Criminal justice asks: What law has been broken? Who is responsible? What do they deserve? The *police* lead the investigation; through *prosecution* the guilt or innocence of those responsible is determined by the state; the judge then decides the appropriate *punishment*. These are the 3Ps, or pillars, of our state based justice system. In the aftermath of riots, and other crimes, this is our expected response from the justice system, and this is what our politicians promise: retributive justice. Other forms of justice ask different questions.

Restorative justice asks: Who has been hurt? What are their needs? Whose obligations are these? The focus shifts from the law, and those who enforce it, to the people and the community affected by the harm. Restorative justice is community born and community led. Crime is viewed as a violation of people, relationships and communities. Those violations create obligations. The central focus shifts from punishing the bad apple, to addressing victim needs, and inviting responsibility for repairing the harm done to victims and communities.

Restorative justice invites us to step up to a justice platform that fosters *respect*, *responsibility* and *resolution* to *repair* the harm done – the 4Rs of community based justice. State and community based justice can work hand in hand, within the standards established by the convention of human rights and the rule of law. This is particularly poignant in the aftermath of riots, given that along with direct harm caused to individuals and businesses, there is a significant level of community harm; in that, the community has been fractured; young people have attacked the social order and harmony of neighbourhoods; the social, emotional, physical and financial cost has been of significant magnitude. The criminal justice system, alone, can only address the issue of guilt or innocence, and hold the individual accountable to the state. Community based restorative justice invites us to take a step deeper into our communities, inviting us to actively participate in what makes us proud to be members of a safe and fully accountable community.

This is the mission of IARS – fostering community led solutions for a fairer society; in other words, to *"give everyone a chance to forge a safer, fairer and more inclusive society"*.

It is a great honour for the Centre for Restorative Justice, at Simon Fraser University in Vancouver, Canada, to be partnering with IARS to better understand and respond to street group violence, as characterized through riots.

Both Vancouver and England experienced the devastating impact of riots in the summer of 2011. Other cities and countries have also felt the heavy impact of riots, while police and the justice system brace themselves for more. The time is ripe to be asking different questions, building new partnerships, and exploring innovative solutions. This book represents a first step in that direction and opens the door for further partnership and collaboration.

We are forever grateful to the Centre for Dialogue at Simon Fraser University, who opened the first door to this international partnership. Through the generous funding of Bruce and Lis Welch, Dr. Gavrielides was invited to deliver the 2012 Welch Community Dialogue, which engages the community at large with the academic community to explore innovative approaches to local community issues through cross-sectoral dialogue. Riots, in both Vancouver and England, was the common community concern. This book uses findings from this visit and Gavrielides' research with communities in Vancouver, England and elsewhere.

Vancouver's riot has many parallels to the British experience, including a desire to provide victims with a better sense of reparation and closure, as well as an interest in reducing the risk of re-offense. Spontaneous responses to the riot demonstrated a desire from community members to participate with officials in the process of ensuring accountability, bridge building, and restoring the social fabric of the affected areas.

While in Vancouver, Dr. Gavrielides met with the media, justice officials, community based groups and the Downtown Vancouver Business Improvement Association. In doing so, Vancouver turned an important page in building understanding of what it means to foster a safer and more fully accountable city.

It takes courage and compassion to turn a new page towards a safer and more inclusive society. Riots cause serious harm to social order and harmony. They are both a threat and an opportunity. They challenge us to ask deeper and different questions about who we are and who we want to be, as individuals and communities. In doing so, riots challenge our understanding of our common humanity and what it takes to live and work in a community that fosters justice for all.

July 2012

Brenda Morrison

5

Preface: Professor Vasso Artinopoulou, Panteion University of Social & Political Sciences

I t is a pleasure to introduce Gavrielides' new study on street group violence and restorative justice. I was not surprised by the research topic, as I am aware of his challenging scientific character and his tendency to 'push the barriers' of restorative justice. Nevertheless, I was pleasantly surprised by the framework of his analysis, the adopted methodology, the international dimension of the work, and his synthesis of transformative/ innovative justice. These issues were well placed within the reality of our complex, modern societies. Until recently, street group violence was perceived in terms of protests, demonstrations and new social movements. Political sciences, sociology and social psychology were the mainstream fields of social sciences, which have traditionally dealt with these phenomena. From A. Tourain theory on new social movements (as collective reactions in new forms of repression, which represent the crisis of traditional paradigms), to criminological approaches on violence and vandalism, there are many definitions moved from general theoretical approaches to more specific and concrete in social contexts. Furthermore, street group violence, as a field of research, was rather 'an autonomous issue', not often studied in an interdisciplinary manner.

Street group violence is often perceived as illegal violence by police or as an extreme form of demonstration by members of the public (often, the oppressed). Theory and research done in the fiends of law and criminology have so far concentrated on the legal dimension and criteria surrounding this violation. The discipline of human rights has also helped us frame police powers and set up standards for state power and control. There can be no doubt, that criminology and law have studied these matters extensively. A gap, nonetheless, still persists.

On the other hand, despite its long practice and history in different cultures and societies, restorative justice in the context of criminology gained identity, theoretical foundations, research findings and policy practices only recently. As a criminological paradigm, restorative justice is largely restricted to juveniles, and in minor cases of interpersonal crime.

What is now attempted by this IARS publication is not only an innovative approach in restorative justice, but also a step forward in social sciences. The research deals with the autonomous issues of street group violence and restorative justice, not in parallel, but in an extremely constructive way. Gavrielides moves with scientific discretion in all corners of restorative justice and criminology, putting the issue of street group violence in the heart of restorative justice theory, research and practice. Gavrielides designs the framework of his analysis with clarity, putting his arguments in the context of real case studies from around the world. With scientific validity, he describes the restorative justice framework, in a broad way and then adapts it for street group violence. At the same time, he considers the political barriers interfering with restorative justice and serious violence. Community bonds, victims and offenders as collective subjects and actors, social healing and restoration of harm are all critical issues that are explored in this publication. The research also looks at restorative justice not merely as a practice, but as a paradigm for dealing with crime and the violation of human relationships.

As the interest in restorative justice continues to grow, evidence based policy is the only way forward and this study offers a good illustration of how this can be achieved. Moreover, restorative justice practices must be examined within an interdisciplinary framework linking the well-established discourses of criminology, law, sociology and political sciences. Gavrielides, being systematic and strict with his research material/cases, focuses only on qualitative research. This is done successfully as generalisations of findings are avoided. At the same time, the research opens up the scientific dialogue as to the boarders and challenges of restorative justice and street group violence. Policymaking and practice are the key areas of contribution of this timely publication, as it brings up the broad spectrum of interventions and restorative practices, formal and/or informal. The question of the appropriateness of restorative justice is still open, and has to remain open.

The strength of restorative justice lies within communities. Its further development must be informed by these communities in a genuine manner. This research and IARS' mission for community-led solutions to current social problems helps us, academics, to develop new lines of thoughts and methods of research and scientific dialogue. This research proposes pilots for dealing with street group violence via restorative justice. The proposed framework for these pilots is applicable internationally including my own country, Greece, where riots have become a common phenomenon due to the financial crisis that we are facing. We are all in desperate need of innovative approaches to crime, and this research takes a bold step in exploring new ways of dealing with street group violence.

June 2012

Vasso Artinopoulou

Waves of Healing

Problem Statement & Research Methodology

I t should not be surprising as to why restorative justice (RJ) has become a popular concept for reformers and researchers craving more holistic and indeed economical approaches to what we call *inter-personal crime*. The practices that come under the banner of RJ are all characterised with a strong element of parties' empowerment in dealing and indeed leading on the restoration of harm and wrongdoing – to the extent possible (Braithwaite, 2002a). For instance, recent research into domestic violence cases that were referred to an RJ intervention post-conviction showed that although the relationship between the two individuals was not always restored, the mere fact that women felt empowered helped to create in them a sense of justice and "the ability to move on" (Pelikan, 2012).

It is not the intention of this paper to discuss the dangers, advantages, safeguards and caveats surrounding RJ's application with *inter-personal* incidents of harm. Our focus is RJ with *group violence*. However, we were not interested in incidents of group violence such as genocide and war. There is a rich literature on the contribution, advantages and disadvantages of RJ-based interventions to this type of group violence including the examples of the Truth and Reconciliation Commissions that were established post the genocides and conflicts in Rwanda (see Kohen *et al*, 2011), Siera Leone (see Park, 2010), former Yugoslavia (see Clark, 2008), Cambodia (e.g. Dicklitch and Malik, 2010), sub-Saharan Africa (Roper and Barria, 2009), Bosnia and Herzegovina and South Africa (e.g. Valiñas and Vanspauwen, 2009).

The focus of this book is RJ's potential, and indeed viability, with *street violence* that involves *groups* of victims and offenders. Our research asked how can RJ's underlying principles be applied in the context of street group violence (e.g. riots) where more than one victim and offender are involved? Does the phenomenon of street group violence present a good opportunity for applying RJ? Why? Why not? If RJ's core values of empowerment, dialogue, voluntariness, honesty, fairness and dignity are to be respected (McCold, 1999; Braithwaite, 2002a; Morrison, 2003; Gavrielides, 2012a), then how can these be communicated to and applied with large groups of offenders and victims? How can equity and fairness for the individual be extended to the community? How can groups of riot offenders come together and collectively enter into a restorative process and dialogue with their group victims? Are there any examples of such restorative practices? Are there any benefits to be gained for group victims and the community, and how can group riot offenders' honesty and commitment be monitored and supported?

9

To provide insights into such complex and difficult questions, this paper carried out case study research by looking at four street group violence events that provided material for either carrying out an RJ intervention or for requesting one. Identifying these case studies was extremely difficult. Indeed the rhetoric that is being developed following recent riots, such as those in August 2011 in England, is rich and the claims for a better resolution through RJ are plenty. Tracking down actual cases proved more difficult than originally anticipated. What proved impossible was identifying cases that had been measured and evaluated. This was due to the recent nature of these events, most of which are still being investigated.

From the outset, it has to be accepted that the qualitative findings of this paper are interim and limited. They are merely intended to spark a new debate in this grey area of policy and practice and the conclusions should not be taken as universal truths. As many critics of the case study method have pointed out, the study of a small number of focused cases can offer no grounds for establishing reliability or generality of findings (Eisenhardt, 1989; Hamel, 1993). Some have even dismissed the case study method altogether, as they believe that the intense exposure of a case biases findings (Stake, 1995).

On the other hand, within social science and criminology, case study research is used extensively, and a number of proponents such as Simons (1980), Stake (1995) and Yin (1984) argue that it can provide the perfect tool for examining contemporary real-life situations. It can also allow for the drilling down into complex issues, and can provide the basis for the application of ideas and extension of methods. This method, combined with in-depth, semi-structured expert interviews and desk research, provided the tools for the book's data collection.

Four recent events of street group violence were selected for investigation. These are the 2011 summer riots in England and Canada (Vancouver), the 2002 riots in India (Gujarat) and the on-going 2010-12 street disturbances in Greece. Although the reasons behind these riots are different, they all fell under our definition of street group violence, as this will later be explained.

The research was conducted in three stages. The first stage involved a preliminary small-scale qualitative survey with unstructured interviews with an expert sample of twelve individuals (three for each examined country). The experts were selected based on the detailed knowledge that they had developed around the examined disturbances in their respective countries. While some of this expertise was gained through research and policy analysis, the majority of participants were practitioners who had worked or are still working directly with rioters and victims affected by the examined events. The findings from the first research stage led to the identification of restorative practices that have been, or are being, developed for the investigated four events. These examples varied in nature, intended impact, and chronology.

In the case of India, the identified project had been known in the literature for some time and hence a follow up literature review was carried out. However, since the available material was limited, follow up interviews were also carried out with two practitioners who had been involved in the identified project. In the case of England, the findings were rather encouraging as various current practices were identified and analysed through four follow up interviews. No literature has yet developed on these examples. In the case of Canada and Greece, follow up interviews with two experts respectively were carried out. In the case of Canada, two further interviews with victim representatives were also completed as well as two with a rioter and the mother of a rioter. Stage 3 involved a data display and critical analysis. Table 1 (overleaf) summarises the methods used.

The book will now proceed with an account of these varied cases. While some of them give examples of how RJ can appear in the resolution of street group violence, others expose key issues of policy, public perception and understanding of RJ and the phenomenon of street group violence. While providing this analysis, the intention was not to speak for or against RJ, but to unravel questions that may shed light in the grey area of bringing group victims and rioters together, while attempting to restore the harm caused to the community and businesses.

It is encouraging that organisations, such as the World Health Organization (WHO) believe that group violence and violence more generally is preventable. They do move on to ask though, "If violence is largely preventable, the question arises: why are there not more efforts to prevent it, particularly at national or provincial and state level .... A major obstacle is simply an absence of knowledge" (World Health Organisation, 2002: 17). This book aims to start a debate that will bridge this gap in knowledge.

Table 1: Project Research Stages

Research Stages	Research Method	Detail
Stage 1 – preliminary fieldwork	12 unstructured expert interviews	3 interviewees from England, Canada, India, Greece
Stage 2 – desk research and follow up fieldwork	Desk research and 2 semi-structured expert interviews	In relation to the December 1992 and February 2002 riots in Gujarat, India
	4 semi-structured expert interviews	In relation to the August 2011 riots in England
	2 semi-structured expert interviews	In relation to the June 2011 riots in Vancouver, Canada
	2 semi-structured expert interviews	In relation to the 2010-12 riots in Greece
	2 semi-structure interviews with victim representatives	In relation to the June 2011 riots in Vancouver, Canada
	2 semi-structure interviews with a rioter and the mother of a rioter	In relation to the June 2011 riots in Vancouver, Canada
Stage 3 – data display and critical analysis	Content Analysis	Analysis of data in a systematic and replicable manner based on predefined categories. Categorisation of the phenomena of interest and the adoption of an interpretive approach to the codified categories (Bryman, 2004)

Definitions: "Restorative Justice" & "Street Group violence"

Definitions can be artificial and run the risk of becoming obsolete very quickly, particularly if they refer to continuously evolving concepts such as RJ and street group violence. While bearing this in mind, a glance at the extant literature will render a number of definitions for RJ (e.g. see Marshall, 1999; Braithwaite, 2002b; Gavrielides, 2008; Johnstone & Ness, 2011). Morrison (2006) argues that RJ has been conceived in two broad ways. One is a *process conception*; the other is a *values conception*. The process conception is characterized by a process that brings together all parties affected by harm or wrongdoing. It is generally accepted that RJ practices consist of direct and indirect mediation, family group conferences, healing/sentencing circles and community restorative boards (Bazemore & Walgrave 1998; Crawford & Newburn, 2003; Gavrielides, 2007). The values conception, on the other hand, is characterised by a set of values, or principles, that distinguish RJ from traditional punitive state justice.

For the purposes of this book, we accept that RJ is "an ethos with practical goals, among which is to restore harm by including affected parties in a (direct or indirect) encounter and a process of understanding through voluntary and honest dialogue" (Gavrielides, 2007: 139). Gavrielides argues that RJ "adopts a fresh approach to conflicts and their control, retaining at the same time certain rehabilitative goals" (ibid). For Braithwaite (2002a) and McCold (1999), the principles underlying this "ethos" are victim reparation, offender responsibility and communities of care. McCold argues that if attention is not paid to all three concerns, then the result will only be partially restorative. Braithwate (2002a) spoke about three groups of RJ principles: constraining, maximising and emergent. Constraining standards specify precise rights and limits, maximising standards pursue restoration and justify the constraining standards and emergent standards are gifts that are given in the process of RJ and may include apology and remorse.

Eglash (1977), to whom the name "restorative justice" is attributed, distinguished three types of criminal justice: *retributive, distributive* and *restorative*. He claimed that the first two focus on the criminal act, deny victim participation in the justice process, and require merely passive participation by offenders. The third one, however, focuses on restoring the harmful effects of these actions, and actively involves all parties in the criminal process. RJ, he said, provides: "a

13

deliberate opportunity for offender and victim to restore their relationship, along with a chance for the offender to come up with a means to repair the harm done to the victim" (Eglash, 1977: 101).

Christie (1977) argued that RJ returns *conflicts as property* to individuals and communities, taking them away from the state and lawyers. He argued that the state has stolen the conflict between citizens, and that this has deprived society of the opportunities for norm-classification. Zehr (1990) spoke about the transformative potential of RJ and its changing lenses of how we view crime. He saw crime as a wound in human relationships, and as an action that "creates an obligation to restore and repair" (Zehr, 1990: 187). He contrasted RJ with the retributive way of defining crime. He argued that retributive justice understands crime as "a violation of the state, defined by law-breaking and guilt. Justice determines blame and administers pain in a contest between the offender and the state directed by systematic rules" (Zehr, 1990: 181).

According to Zehr, RJ sees crime as a conflict not between the individual and the state, but between individuals. Accordingly, this understanding encourages the victim and the offender to see one another as persons. In consequence, the focus of the process is on the restoration of human bonds, and the reunion of the two individuals that have been affected by harm or of the individual with their community. As he pointed out, this understanding of crime "creates an obligation to make things right", and while "retributive justice focuses on the violation of state law...RJ focuses on the violation of people and relationships" (Zehr, 1990: 199). In a similar vein, Sharpe claims that RJ "puts its energy into the future, not into what is past. It focuses on what needs to be healed, what needs to be repaired, what needs to be learned in the wake of a crime. It looks at what needs to be strengthened if such things are not to happen again" (1998: 45).

Moving on to the extant literature on *street group violence*, we noticed that it principally focused on criminal gangs and the various definitions and factors that are associated with them (e.g. see Maguire et al, 2007). This paper will not engage with this debate. As it will be argued, *group violence* is not synonymous to *gang violence*. The debate on street group violence and the available literature is rather thin. Hence the understanding of what this term encompasses is only just developing.

This was well reflected in our interviews. For instance, one practitioner said, "It's hard to define as an entity". One of our interviewed experts also said, "Street group violence is a broad and vague term. For, 'street' means public space; 'group' definitions need further adjectives such as age (e.g. 'youth group'), ethnicity (minorities group), gender, culture (subculture groups) etc., and also 'violence' need to be addressed as its forms and types (physical violence, by whom, define offenders and victims)". Someone else added: "Within a theoretical context street group violence, however you choose to operationalize it, resembles mobbing or herding behaviour. It is predictable. Anonymity, to a naive degree, allows for the expression (by some) of anti-social behaviour...see for instance the riots in Athens, Vancouver, etc."

Looking at the term *street violence*, it generally refers to the use of physical force by individuals or groups within public spaces, the result of which may involve injury or death (Anderson, 1999). Turning our focus exclusively on the word *violence*, this is typically categorized according to the relationship between the victim and the perpetrator, as well as the location in which it takes place (Rosenberg *et al,* 1992). The WHO defines violence as "The intentional use of physical force or power, threatened or actual, against oneself, another person, or against a group or community that either results in or has a high likelihood of resulting in injury, death, psychological harm, maldevelopment or deprivation" (World Health Organisation, 2002: 5).

The WHO (2002) accepts three broad categories of violence. These are based on the characteristics of those committing the violent act: (1) self-directed violence (2) interpersonal violence (3) collective violence or, as named in this paper, group violence. According to the WHO, collective or group violence is subdivided into social, political and economic violence.

By definition, *group violence* is committed by large groups of individuals, which can be previously related or not, or by states. As Kelly (2000) points out, although group violence often involves acts of individual violence, it is distinguished from violence that occurs between individuals who do not act as part of, or on behalf of, particular groups. According to the literature, there are various reasons for committing group violence. These include:

● advancing a particular social agenda (e.g. terrorist acts, mob violence, hate crime),
● promoting political violence (e.g. war and related violent conflict, state violence and similar acts carried out by large groups such as paramilitaries), and
● spreading economic violence (e.g. attacks disturbing economic activity, denying access to essential services or creating economic division and fragmentation).

Types of group violence are, of course, war and genocide. These have been the subject of research and political debates for some time, and there are numerous scientific studies on their underlying causes. For instance, Bigelow (1969), Le Blanc (2003), Thayer (2004) and Gat (2006) believe that it is in our nature to commit atrocities of collective violence. Durrant summarises this view: "The seeming ubiquity of war, genocide, and other forms of group conflict in human history has led many scholars to conclude that our capacity for collective violence is firmly rooted in the evolutionary history of our species" (2011: 428). This paper will not engage with this type of group violence.

This book's focus is *group violence* that occurs on the streets, and is unilateral, time-bound and non-governmental. According to de la Roche, this type of group violence is usually observed in the following four phenomena: riots, lynching, vigilantism and terrorism and each is " distinguished by its system of liability and degree of organisation" (1996: 97). The term group is defined here as per Olzak (1992) and Tilly (1978), encompassing five or more people acting in concert.

One of the interviewed practitioners for our study asked, "What is the difference between multiple violent events and the riot phenomenon?" The same practitioner went on to say, "I have been involved in most of the serious riots in the UK from the late 60s to the late 80s. The one striking factor that I have noticed is that there is a moment when the crowd of individuals, often individually violent or threatening, does change to a riotous mob with an almost concerted joint action and a loss of individual choice or control".

In our definition, it is also important to include deviant behaviour that, according to de la Roche, is not merely conduct that "an outside observer might regard as odd, abnormal, or illegal, but any action – however seemingly trivial, inoffensive, or innocent – that is subject to social control" (1996: 98). The literature from psychology, sociology, criminology and economics is extensive in helping us to understand the various reasons underlying this type of group violence. For some, this violence appears to be more rational and comprehensible than that of others. For instance, some have argued that if carried out by economically and socially subordinate groups, such as the unemployed, working classes, minority groups and disadvantaged youth, then the action may be reasonable and possibly even worthy of sympathetic understanding from the top down and by dominant groups (e.g. see Tilly et al, 1975 and Fogelson, 1970).

One of our interviewees noted, "I understand street group violence involving groups of persons on the street who engage in threatening or violent behaviour. Most of the times, these people will commit serious offences against the Public

Order Act 1986. We have to accept that society has declared such behaviour as unacceptable, as a criminal offence; then we can make further progress on the matter. The law has always set out that individuals are responsible for their own actions. Being part of a group is held to be an aggravating factor and this is reflected in the seriousness of the offences and the associated penalties".

Mattaini and Strickland (2006) explored the roots of this violence from the perspective of the natural science of behaviour. They argue, "Strategies for modifying collective violence should take into consideration motivational factors such as verbal processes and cultural perceptions, shifting motivating antecedents, etc. Rules, models, and structural conditions are also relevant" (ibid: 500). There are many theories and paradigms aiming to provide explanations for group violence. It is not the intention of this paper to provide an analysis of these views. However, it is important to acknowledge their existence.

Street Group Violence: Four events

Event no 1: **England, August 2011**

Sparked by the shooting of 29 year old Mark Duggan by police in Tottenham on 6th August 2011, 12 London areas and 66 other locations in England experienced looting, physical violence and damage, arson, theft and robbery. The riots across England lasted for five continuous days. Five people lost their lives and hundreds more lost their businesses and homes. The financial loss is estimated to be £1 billion.[1] In summary, the crimes that were committed were:

- **Violence against the individual**: e.g. the Metropolitan Police reported 2175 injuries, and West Midlands Police reported 296.
- **Arson**: e.g. in London, 171 residential buildings and 100 commercial buildings were affected by fire. In some other areas, cars and bins were set alight, sometimes to create barriers against police intervention.
- **Criminal damage**: e.g. in London, thousands of shops were damaged and over 3,800 claims were recorded under the Riot (Damages) Act 1886.
- **Theft**: e.g. high value consumer and electrical products (e.g. phones and computers).

The media largely reported the events as youth disturbances, while programmes were repeatedly played on national TV and radio about a declining morality among Britain's youth. On the one hand, the current Prime Minister (David Cameron) was talking about "a moral decline, deep-seated problems of thuggery, selfishness and greed", and on the other hand the ex-Prime Minister (Tony Blair) was pointing the finger at "a small core of families living outside all social norms and substituting feral gangs for society".[2]

The UK coalition government was swift and tough in its response, with its Prime Minister addressing the rioters: "You will feel the full force of the law and if you are old enough to commit these crimes you are old enough to face the punishment".[3] As of February 2011, it is estimated that 13,000 - 15,000 people were actively involved in the riots and more than 4,000 suspected rioters have been arrested (Riots, Communities and Victims Panel, 2012). In particular, Ministry of Justice (MoJ) data shows that by 12 October 2011, 1,984 defendants had appeared before the courts for crimes committed during the riots. They were: 90% males; 26% aged 10–17; 27% aged 18–20; 21% aged 21–24; 5% aged over 40; 42% were White, 46% were Black, 7% were Asian and 5% were Other. At the time when these statistics were published, 1,362 (69%) of the defendants had not received a final outcome at court. The remaining 622 (31%) had received a final outcome, of which 331 (53%) had received a custodial sentence, 220 (35%) received a sentence other than custody and 71 (11%) were either acquitted or had their case dismissed.[4]

Soon after the event, a considerable amount of resource was spent in setting up and maintaining the Independent Riots, Communities and Victims Panel tasked with examining and understanding why the August 2011 riots took place. Following a national call for evidence, an Interim report was published in November 2011. The final report was published in March 2012 setting out "final findings and recommendations for action to help prevent future riots".[5] This report is just one of several, investigating the causes of the riots.[6] It is not within the remit of this paper to analyse their findings. Indicatively, some of the causes that they identified include, "When people feel they have no reason to stay out of trouble the consequences can be devastating. We must give everyone a stake in society" (Riots, Communities and Victims Panel, 2012: 6). Interestingly, both the interim and final reports by the Independent Riots, Communities and Victims Panel recommended RJ. Various other reports were then published by think-tank and pressure groups (e.g. see Morrell et al, 2011).

Event no 2: India, December 1992 and February 2002

Following the destruction of Babri Masjid, a 16th century mosque, large groups of Muslims reacted to the Hindu nationalist claim that the mosque stood on a site sacred to the Hindu god Rama. Riots were provoked in six states across India. These events bruit for some time when finally in February 2002 street group violence occurred in Gujarat. 58 Hindu Ram sevaks were burned to death on their way from Babri. In retaliation, 2000 men, women and children were raped, killed or burned alive and more than 200,000 people were made homeless or saw their businesses brought to the ground (Powers, 2008; Harsh, 2004).

According to Ahmed, "thousands of Muslim families moved to relief camps in urban areas largely maintained by various Islamic committees" (2004: 95). Harsh (2003) describes the spreading of the riots to 151 towns and 993 villages across India. He explains how Hindus and Muslims withdrew from the mixed communities in which they had been living for years and how trust quickly broke down.

The reaction of the Chief Minister was swift and punitive; "I want to assure people that Gujarat shall not tolerate any such incident. The culprits will get full punishment for their sins. Not only this, we will set an example, that nobody not even in his dreams, thinks of committing a heinous crime like this" (Narenda Modi, Chief Minister, on State television on 28 February 2002, cited in Varadarajan, 2002).

Nonetheless, no one has been convicted of involvement in the atrocities yet (Ahmed, 2004: 95). According to Ahmed, thousands have been detained, but justice and reconciliation is yet to be achieved. Community relations remain tense, and conflict, suspicion and in many instances hatred affect the two communities. While there has been some financial reparation by the state and national Indian governments, the affected victims still perceive a level of injustice and a lack of resolution (PUCL, 2002).

To date, there hasn't been any independent review of the Gujarat riots. Various scholars and NGOs have attempted to research the causes, and help create an understanding (e.g. see Helie *et al*, 2003). One such example is the research carried out by Shankar and Gerstein (2007). Their small qualitative study involved "a few Hindus and Muslims affected by the violence in Gujarat to tell their stories and solutions for peace building in their neighbourhoods" (Helie *et al,* 2003: 374). Conditions such as economic prosperity, political conflicts, social polarisation and segregation were mentioned as key causes. Explanatory riot theories such as the Realistic Group Conflict Theory (Sherif, 1966), Social Identity Theory (Tajfel and Turner, 1986) and Contract Hypothesis Theory (Allport, 1954) were tested. Shankar and Gerstein conclude in their research: "Some of the injustices shared by the current participants focus on the perpetrators of violence in Gujarat who continue to evade punishment for crimes they committed" (2007: 376).

Event no 3: **Vancouver, June 2011**

In June 2011, Vancouver was faced with serious street group disturbances and riots. Following the Boston Bruins win over the Vancouver Canucks for the Stanley Cup, angry fans caused criminal damages and committed street group violence. At least 140 people were reported as injured during the events, one critically; at least four people were stabbed, nine police officers were injured, and 101 people were arrested that night, with 16 further arrests following the event. 89 businesses were badly affected and 113 vehicles were damaged. In total, there were 299 criminal incidents and 43 assaults. It is estimated that the total costs of the riots will be more than $5 million CAD.[7]

On June 20, 2011 the Province, the City of Vancouver and the Vancouver Police Board announced an independent review of the planning and activities that led up to, and the violence that followed, the Stanley Cup final game. On 31 August 2011, the Final Report was published.[8] Interestingly, the report notes: "The question then is not the cause of the riot – troublemakers deliberately caused it – but the conditions that gave them the opportunity. The key ingredients were congestion and free flowing alcohol" (Furlong and Keefe, 2011:1).

On 18th April 2012, the Integrated Riot Investigation Team presented its findings to the Vancouver Police Board. 508 charges were made, 225 of which had been approved. The up to date cost of the investigation was estimated at around $9 million CAD. Police investigators are still working through 5,500 hours of video footage and 65,000 tagged people.[9]

Event no 4: **Greece, 2010-12**

Since May 2010, there has been an ongoing series of street group disturbances across Greece, sparked by the enforced austerity measures and the plans to cut public spending and raise further taxes in response to the Greek debt crisis.

On 5th May 2010, protests took place in Athens resulting in three people being killed and many businesses destroyed. On 25th May 2011, riots spread in various major cities across the country. On 29th June 2011, violent clashes occurred in Athens between the riot police and protesters as the Greek parliament voted to accept the EU's austerity requirements.

In February 2012, ahead of a historic vote in Parliament on additional austerity measures, more than 120 people were hurt in new rioting in Athens, which also broke out in other cities. Clashes erupted after more than 500,000 protesters marched to Parliament to rally against the drastic cuts. In total 45 buildings were set ablaze and at least 70 protesters were also hospitalized. Police arrested at least 67 people, while in several cases they had to escort fire crews to burning buildings after protesters prevented access.[10] Authorities said 68 police needed medical care. On April 5th 2012, further riots took place following a pensioner's suicidal message, "I will not follow the same fate as of those searching for food in garbage".[11] The riots are expected to continue.

Chapter Notes

1 This includes £300 million claims under the Riots (Damages) Act 1886, £30 million in lost sales, £50 million costs to the police and so on (Riots, Communities and Victims Panel, 2012). Furthermore, 330,000 tourists have been predicted to go elsewhere, cutting tourism spending by £520m over a 12 month period.

2 (Accessed September 2011) http://www.guardian.co.uk/politics/blog/2011/aug/22/tony-blair-riot-remedy-feral-families

3 (Accessed September 2011) http://www.telegraph.co.uk/news/uknews/crime/8691034/London-riots-Prime-Ministers-statement-in-full.html

4 (Accessed October 2011) http://www.bbc.co.uk/news/uk-14931987

5 (Accessed April 2012) http://riotspanel.independent.gov.uk/ The final and interim report can also be downloaded.

6 See for instance a plethora of reports published by Reading the Riots, a partnership between the newspaper The Guardian and The London School of Economics and Political Sciences (accessed 2012) http://www.guardian.co.uk/uk/london-riots

7 http://www.cbc.ca/news/canada/british-columbia/story/2011/10/31/bc-vancouver-riot-charges.html

8 The report can be downloaded from http://www.pssg.gov.bc.ca/vancouverriotreview/ (accessed April 2012).

9 (Accessed April 2012) http://vancouver.ca/police/2011riot/index.html

10 "Clashes erupt as Greek Parliament debates austerity measures". CNN. 12 February 2012. http://edition.cnn.com/2012/02/12/world/europe/greece-debt-crisis/index.html. Retrieved 12 February 2012.

11 (Accessed April 2012) http://rt.com/news/greece-protest-pensioner-suicide-306

Restorative Justice with Street Group Violence

Case study no 1: England – restorative justice through the criminal justice system

The first RJ example from England is being offered through the criminal justice system to both adults and juveniles convicted of riot related offences. It is worth noting that in England and Wales, the criminal justice system has four key sub-systems: (1) Law enforcement (Police & Prosecution), (2) Courts, (3) Penal System (Probation & Prisons) and (4) Crime Prevention. The identified example exists only within the Greater Manchester area and is implemented by the Greater Manchester Probation Trust (GMPT). In a bid "to meet the changing needs of sentencers and victims",[12] GMPT quickly developed a new intervention for courts called the Intensive Citizenship, Responsibility and Consequences order (I-CRC). Within this initiative, an RJ intervention is provided.

The I-CRC is based on the Intensive Alternative to Custody (IAC) programme, which has been offered by GMPT since April 2009. IAC aims to offer a robust community-based intervention that helps reduce the harm that male offenders of 18-25 years of age cause to the community. IAC is an alternative to custody for offenders who would normally receive a prison sentence of less than 12 months.

The I-CRC is a Community Order that is offered by GMPT as an intensive alternative to custody sentencing option for those offenders specifically convicted as a result of the 2011 street group violence. It has been designed especially for sentenced rioters whether male or female, juveniles or adults. It is intended to act as an additional sentencing option for courts, or as an option for cases where there has been a successful appeal against the original custodial sentence. According to the interviewed expert who manages this programme, the Order can have an impact on sentencing outcomes. In cases that go to the Crown, I-CRC is followed through a regular Progress Report. In particular, the I-CRC consists of four modules:

(1) Curfew for 3 months[13]
(2) Community Payback[14]
(3) Four sessions of a rehabilitation and responsibility programme delivered in a group setting and focused on street group violence and its consequences

(4) Followed by three sessions of RJ delivered on a one-to-one basis and linked to community panels focusing on apology, accountability and restoration.

Looking closer at module 3, this consists of four group sessions with related riot offenders. Session 1 ("What Happened") looks at the events before and during the August street group violence and what could have been done differently for the offenders not to get involved. Session 2 ("In the Heat of the Moment?") explores the psychological aspects of offenders' involvement including emotions, self-control and impulsivity. Particular attention is given to addressing psychological aspects relating to group offenders who often report not feeling that emotional control was an issue. Session 3 ("Who Suffers") aims to prepare the three follow up RJ sessions by bringing the victim's perspective, and by starting a dialogue on the impact of the participants' street group violence actions on group victims and the community. Finally, Session 4 ("What Now") aims to encourage offenders to start assessing the impact of their actions on their immediate and long-term personal futures. Again, looking at offenders as a group, the Session assesses the balance of pro-social to pro-criminal attitudes within each group in question. The Session rounds up with individual statements of intent and a summary identifying the rights and collective responsibilities of the individual as a citizen.

Alongside module 3, the victim awareness probation officer works on a one to one and group basis with riot offenders to increase, and on many occasions instil, a sense of victim empathy. This involves three sessions that are run in conjunction with I-CRC. Table 2 (adapted from a GMPT unpublished document), outlines the key aims and features of these sessions.

Moving onto the 4th module of RJ, this is done on a one-to-one basis via face-to-face conferencing which includes the affected victim. One of our interviewed practitioners pointed out that there are more chances of success if the offenders are separated and are not grouped together when meeting the victim. The practitioner noted: "Having three or five related rioters in one meeting, runs the risk of intimidating the victim. Grouping offenders is possible, but it demands a lot of preparation in making sure that the right balance is struck". The practitioner also noted: "If the rioters are grouped together in the same RJ session, they tend to talk generally about the impact of their actions avoiding personal responsibility taking. They tend to hide behind others' actions". Interestingly, it was also noted that although IAC, on which the Order was based, has been applied with co-defendants successfully, this has not been the case for group crimes.

It is worth noting that while the group sessions of module 3 are delivered by

Table 2: Greater Manchester Probation Trust Victim Awareness Delivery Model (© GMPT 2012)

Session	1. Ripple effect	2. Perspective Taking	3. Remorse & Responsibility
Aim	To discuss and acknowledge the breadth of impact their actions have and identify all potential victims	To hone in on particular victims, understand their perspective, improve empathy, encourage first feelings of remorse	To demonstrate remorse, acknowledge responsibility and do something about it; to make right that wrong[15]
Exercises (choose one of the following from each section)	• Ripple effect using cards • Ripple effect on paper • Victim tick list • Ball of string exercise (if doing in a group)	• Victim TFB/ABC • Victim case study • When I was a victim exercise • Writing letter from victim's perspective and saying to camera	• Accountability letter • Apology letter • Restorative justice worksheet

probation trained staff, the RJ intervention is carried out through a partnership model which may involve an RJ trained probation or police officer or a community-based mediation service. The interviewed practitioners pointed out that additional community services also tend to get involved, such as victim support agencies which provide checks and balances for the victim. Other community organisations may offer support systems for the offenders who tend to find themselves in an emotional and transformative cycle of guilt, repentance and reintegration.

Talking about a specific case that had completed module 3 and was about to enter the 4th module (RJ), one interviewed practitioner pointed out, "Although I will be one of the participants in the conferencing sessions, I will not be the facilitator. Our trained police officer will now lead the process". The case involved a young rioter convicted of criminal damage against a large chain shop. The victim-business was represented by the store manager as well as the security guard. Other parties who were invited to take part in the RJ sessions were the offender's family, the victim awareness probation officer, a nearby resident and an impartial transcriber. The venue that was chosen was the shopping centre where the offence had taken place. The practitioner pointed out: "We don't just proceed with this stage without proper and thorough risk assessment. Also this stage is well prepared with several sessions of victim awareness over 4-5 weeks of one-to-one meetings with the delegated victim awareness probation officer". The victim is also well prepared by the RJ practitioner; "No one participates if they are not truly willing and indeed prepared", they said.

The I-CRC has a supervision requirement for 3 months in order to promote compliance. During this period, referrals to employment and training programmes are also made. Understandably, it is too early for the I-CRC to safely claim success. While evaluation and monitoring is being carried out as part of normal procedures within the Trust, thinking is also being developed for a more focused RJ research project.[16]

Follow up interviews with the GMPT senior management team revealed an additional case study with a young rioter. The practitioner said, "The case study relates to offences that were committed during the 9th and 10th August 2011 riots. They involved theft (large quantity of cigarettes), criminal damage and possession of cannabis. In commission of the offence, the rioter threw a large item through a window of a store in a shopping centre. He was intoxicated when the offences were committed. He admitted that he had been drinking with peers who he reports were egging each other on to get involved in the riot. He was sentenced in January 2012 and had been on remand since then. He was 21 years old when sentenced and 20 when the offences were committed. He had no previous convictions and was in employment when the offence was committed. When we offered the I-CRC he accepted and after successful completion of the three modules we proceeded with an RJ conference in June 2012. He met representatives of the local community who were affected by the riots. This included a representative of the business community, a city centre resident who witnessed the riots and a local city councillor. We received positive feedback from all involved in the conference. One of the outcomes from the conference was that he "gives something back to the city". He is currently producing artwork to promote Manchester and offering to meet offenders to offer advice to assist them to move on from offending. He is now in employment again".

Case study no 2 & 3: **England – restorative justice through the youth justice system**

The second case study from England was offered as part of the formal youth justice system (YJS). It is worth noting that in England and Wales, the criminal justice system is distinct from the YJS, which is characterised by a complex set of arrangements led by the Ministry of Justice.[17] This involves multi agency Youth Offending Teams (YOTs), on a local basis. A brief account of the YJS might assist understanding of the case study.

The main custodial sentence for young people (10-17 at the time of conviction) is the detention and training order. Young people may also be sentenced to extended determinate or indeterminate sentences under Sections 226 and 288 of Criminal Justice Act 2003. The main reform of the YJS took place through the 'Crime and Disorder Act 1998' (CDA), which according to some is the first enabling legislation for RJ in England and Wales (e.g., see Gavrielides, 2007). With its principal aim "the prevention of offending by young people", the Act introduced three central innovative features into the youth justice system.

The first feature was the 'Youth Justice Board for England and Wales' (YJB), an executive non-departmental public body that oversees the youth justice system. It aims to prevent offending and reoffending by children and young people under the age of 18. The second was the 'Youth Offending Teams' (YOTs). These are multi-agency panels formed by local authorities to provide reports for courts, supervise young offenders sentenced by the court, and to undertake preventative work. Their staff includes police officers, social workers, probation officers, education and health workers and youth service officers. Third, the Act introduced a range of new orders and amended existing ones.

The major impact in relation to RJ was the introduction of formal Reprimands and Final Warning. These are applicable for first offences committed by young people and are intended as a diversion from prosecution. They are designed to be delivered in a restorative manner and they call for the victim's views and involvement to be sought. The Final Warning is referred to and delivered by the multi-agency YOT and is the largest restorative response, albeit at an early stage of offending. One specific measure was the 'Reparation Order', which enables courts to order young people to undertake practical reparation activities directly to either victims or the community. This needs to be the outcome of a mutual agreement between the parties. Section 2.4 made it clear that "...it should not be a mechanistic process based upon an eye for eye approach; instead any reparation

29

should be tailored to meet both the needs of the victim, if they wish to be involved and addressing the offending behaviour of the young offender" (Home Office 1998: S2.4). Section 6.1 set down the restorative nature of the outcomes to which such a process should lead. Finally, the guidance notes suggested that victim-offender mediation could be considered as a part of 'Reparation Order', and that YOTs may wish to consider establishing this restorative process (Home Office, 1998: S6.1). RJ is also visible in other elements of the Act such as 'Action Plan Orders', final warnings and reprimands.

The 'Youth Justice and Criminal Evidence Act 1999' (YJCEA) also introduced the 'Referral Order'.[18] This is a mandatory sentence for young offenders (10-17) appearing in court for the first time who have not committed an offence likely to result in custody. The court determines the length of the Order based on the seriousness of the offence, and can last between three and twelve months. Once the sentence length has been decided, the juvenile is referred to a 'Youth Offender Panel' to work out the content of the order. These panels are arranged by local YOTs and can include: the offender and their family and friends, the victim and their family, a representative of the local YOT and three members of the community. In theory, the process is a restorative one, including honest and sincere understanding of what happened and the pain inflicted and what needs to occur to put it right. The Government has described the Order as the first introduction of RJ into the youth justice system, while the Act itself makes specific reference to victim-offender mediation as a possible agreed outcome of a panel.

The Criminal Justice and Immigration Act 2008 introduced the Youth Rehabilitation Order (YRO), which is a generic community sentence for young offenders and combines a number of sentences into one generic sentence. It is now the standard community sentence used for the majority of children and young people who offend. An Activity requirement, or a Supervision requirement can require reparation to a victim and, if agreed a meeting or communication with a victim. This will be the main measure to enable restorative practices with young people who offend at this level.

Moving on to the case study, on the 14th November 2011, the YOT of Lambeth City Council which was heavily affected by the riots, carried out a successful face-to-face meeting between a young offender convicted of taking part in the public disturbances and the manager of a KFC store that was vandalised in the Brixton area. The meeting took place in the Town Hall and had the form of a face-to-face mediation. The local police force and local Councillors were behind the initiative. The Council Cabinet Member for Children and Young People's Service, Councillor

Pete Robbins said publicly: "This programme is about putting victims first, providing them with a voice and reassuring the community that justice is being done. Those convicted of looting and rioting have had a big impact on the lives of their victims and facing up to this fact benefits everyone".[19]

The meeting was requested by the victim-business, which was represented by its manager. The parties were prepared by the YOT staff ensuring that the process was voluntary and complementary. The meeting started with some probing questions by the manager aiming to understand the behaviour and reasons that led the teenager to join the group that vandalised the shop during the street group disturbances. The manager said: "I was willing to speak to the young man to tell him how the attack on KFC Brixton made me and my staff feel. Judging by his reaction a lot of good has come from this – for both of us".

As a result of the meeting, the teenager accepted responsibility, apologised and signed a "moral contract" in which he pledged to see through his reparation activities. These included writing lyrics and a play about his experience of the public disturbances and the RJ process that he had experienced. He also agreed to feed back his experience to his friends and other people involved in the events. The manager offered to mentor him with further one-to-one chats, and meet him more formally again for a follow up mediation. The manager said: "As the programme progressed, I found myself becoming more and more proud of the young person for facing up to his actions".

PC Donna-Marie McKinson, the practitioner behind the initiative said that, "The RJ approach is a great step forward to healing community ties within Lambeth. The young offenders involved will get to hear first-hand how the shop staff themselves and their families were affected; emotionally, financially and physically". Follow up interviews suggested that the Council is looking to expand this practice as part of its campaign "Be Safe" which aims to bring people responsible for the summer street group violence to justice. The case later featured in the final report of the Riots, Communities and Victims Panel (2012).

The third case study appeared in the Riots, Communities and Victims Panel report (2012). This was also carried out within the YJS and it involved five young people who caused extensive damage to a local church in Croydon during the summer riots. They were caught by church staff and arrested for offences of criminal damage and non-domestic burglary. The meeting was organised by the local YOT as part of their *Triage* programme aiming at first time entrants to the YJS who receive their first substantive outcome relating to a reprimand, a final warning or a court disposal. The programme has been running since April 2009 and it "aims to prevent the unnecessary entry of young people into the criminal justice system, to divert these young people at an early stage into effective restorative interventions".[20] After several pre-meetings with the offenders and the affected victim-church who was represented by its Minister, a restorative conference was arranged. This was also attended by the building's manager and the young people's parents. The group offenders were all included on the same session. According to the YOT, the meeting was successful in that the Minister received answers to the questions he was seeking and the young offenders collectively agreed to restore the damages that they had caused to the church during the riots.

Case study no 4: **England – restorative justice through a multi-agency, cross-sector partnerships**

This case study from England was not identified within the formal justice system, but within the community setting. It involves principally a series of group conferences that took place in the area of Southwark (London, England). The initiative focused on the Somali community and young Somali people living within the Borough and it included an inter-community dialogue event, while the riots were taking place. It was the outcome of a multi-agency, cross-sector partnership involving the local authority, The Somali Relief and Islamic Culture Centre, the local mosque, the community-based charity Empowering People for Excellence[21] and the local Metropolitan Police.

According to an interviewed practitioner, the initiative aimed to "ensure that the parents and elders took responsibility for the young people involved in the riots. It was a wonderful demonstration of partnership work in action and how commitment to effective community engagement is important to maintaining good community relations all year round. This is why we believe that the damages to Somali businesses on Old Kent Road was minimal".

The practitioner said to us, "During those 5 days of riots I had mothers coming to me with bags of jewellery begging me to give it back to the police. They were saying that their children wanted to give it back and say sorry. They did not know what they were doing at the time". She carried on to note, "They were just afraid to go to the police. They knew that they would be prosecuted. What is the point here? To prosecute or give the jewellery back and restore the relationships that were broken and the harm that was caused to the community and to businesses?"

The RJ practitioner continued to say, "Communities and residents as stakeholders were denied the opportunities to ask "why me/ my home?", and to be part of a process of community dialogue, healing, restoration and closure. Communities are still seeking reassurance about the riots not occurring again. The criminal justice process prohibited a number of parents coming forward to apologise for their children's actions, to give their account about their children's involvement and their role as parents in repairing the harm done, due to fear, shame, guilt, stigmatisation, the threat of legal action and loss of home. In the homes of many young people in London and the UK there are still lots of jewellery and items that were burgled/ stolen from pawnshops that have not been returned to their owners. These owners simply want their items returned. I am aware of those involved in street gangs who put 'word out' about the return of certain jewellery and the repercussions if this is not done. Because of the criminal justice process and the fact that there has not been an amnesty closure ... healing cannot occur because no dialogue and guidance has been given on these issues from the government or local authorities".

It is worth noting that RJ provision through the community sector is dependent on the given local strategy and the Borough's priorities. Where in some areas examples of good practice are abundant and robust, in some other areas there is complete lack of provision and, on many occasions, hostility, or at least strong scepticism, towards the RJ practice. This is expected as in the UK, RJ developed organically and in the shadow of the law without any formal structures that would mainstream it as a consistent option. This is still the case as the RJ practice is chosen on an *ad hoc* basis by agencies in the public, private and voluntary sectors. Consequently, funding for RJ services has always been a challenge (Gavrielides, 2007). This must also be considered against a background of recent spending cuts.

The lack of formal structure has presented key challenges for RJ practitioners working in the community to prevent and/ or deal with street group violence. One such challenge is receiving referrals of cases and indeed identifying "offenders". Without a solid and well-founded relationship with the local police and Council services (e.g. housing, health and social departments), the process and length of an RJ approach is prolonged. However, one practitioner noted, this difficulty can be overcome by building strong relationships with local people who will then refer the case through word of mouth. "Most of the new users get referred to me by word of mouth. I've got good links in the local community and with the police as I've worked in Southwark for over 11 years, previously as a mediator. I try to address social exclusion, children getting into gangs, parental/child relationship breakdown".

A similar informal initiative within the community was also identified during our research. However, we were unable to follow up any findings because despite the victim's and offenders' willingness to meet, the project was being stalled due to financial restraints. The interviewed practitioner who worked for a London-based voluntary mediation centre pointed out: "We approached the Ministry of Justice for some funding but we were rejected. We cannot do this without any resource at all. We know that restorative justice is more cost effective, and when it works it works really well. The government cannot expect us to provide this for free".

Case study no 5: **India – restorative justice through the community and civil society**

The fifth case study involves an RJ-based intervention that was placed within India's civil society. The identified project did not divert prosecuted cases nor did it reduce sentences. In particular, during the early 2000s, NGOs in Ahmedabad and Vadodara (Baroda) with the assistance of international bodies and donor development agencies, such as CARE,[22] set up civil society projects that would bring Hindus and Muslims together to discuss what happened post the riots. One of these programmes was the Gujarat Harmony Project (GHP) an intervention specifically designed for the rioters and their victims, and based on the RJ paradigm.

The GHP was initiated in May 2002 and was delivered through a partnership of ten diverse development organisations, eight of which are NGOs. All GHP partners were active during the relief phase post the riots and collectively had reach in rural and urban India. They also represented the diverse cultural, gender and religious elements that characterised the affected community-parties. The programme was neither state driven nor was it offered as part of the official criminal justice system.

The key aims of GHP were the rehabilitation of the rioters, the restoration of the victim-communities and the re-establishment of social harmony. According to Ahmed (2004), it involved seven key types of interventions:

(1) Livelihood restoration
(2) Social reconciliation
(3) Habitat security
(4) Psycho-social care
(5) Advocacy to promote social harmony
(6) Community education, and
(7) Knowledge building and documentation.

The strategies and activities to deliver these interventions were diverse and were provided within "a framework of social action" and active citizenship (Smillie and Hailey, 2001: 91). These projects stretched from the provision of basic reconciliation activities such as festival celebrations, school and community learning and training, credit activities, health and sport projects. According to Ahmed, "the core theory of social change underlying the GPH is the principle of RJ" (2004: 97).

In addition to informing the general philosophy of the GHP, RJ was used as a direct intervention. One such example was group conferencing with Hindu and Muslim women who had been affected by the riots. According to Porter (2007), women were the primary target of the riots mainly affected by violence such as rape, bodily mutilation, humiliation, murder and being burned alive. As Mander reports, women's "bodies [became] battlefields to avenge, subjugate and even eliminate an entire community" (2004: 16).

Focusing on sexual and domestic violence, the RJ programmes brought surrogate victims together to encourage understanding, break down stereotypes and help each other heal. Dr. Velahudhan, a practitioner involved in the project, said: "We've cried a lot. We shouted at each other a lot, especially in the beginning stages. But we've bonded and become very close. It's been a process of constant problem-solving, learning as we go".[23]

Ahmed (2004) reports on the findings of an evaluation of the GHP that she was tasked to carry out on behalf of CARE. This was carried out over 20 days in 2004. Focus groups were held with participants and interviews with eight out of the ten organisations driving the GHP. She concludes: "The GHP stands out as an important example of RJ in the face of the failure of the retributive system. Equally important, it illustrates the potential role that outsider agencies can play in facilitating reconciliation through civil society partnerships" (Ahmed, 2004: 95). The programme, however, was also criticised for its "target driven approach". Ahmed reports, "Some partners maintain that the GHP has lost its vitality; that it has been driven by targets rather than processes, and has become just another development programme" (2004: 101).

The qualitative findings of Shankar and Gerstein (2007) are also helpful; "Participants reported they felt responsible for peace initiatives and welcomed opportunities to participate in community building activities in their neighbourhoods" (ibid: 374). Montiel and Wessells (2001), agreed with this finding as they conclude that community-based action initiatives, such as RJ circles and conferences, are more likely to strengthen neighbourhoods against street group violence, especially if such initiatives are direct extensions of the roles community members play in their homes and in the community as peacebuilders. Shankar and Gerstein conclude in their research on Gujarat that, "To assist the Hindu and Muslim communities in Gujarat in achieving justice, models such as the South African Truth and Reconciliation Commission might be employed" (2007: 376). They proceed to clarify that due to the different type of group violence that was experienced in Gujarat, smaller RJ conference style meetings should be pursued at a local level. "Provided there is a commitment to restoring justice in the state of Gujarat, its administration might be able to implement, for example, a series of smaller ad hoc committees in different neighbourhoods" (Shankar and Gerstein 2007: 376). De la Rey (2001) agrees with their recommendation.

Case study no 6: **Requesting restorative justice for the Vancouver riots**

In the case of the 2011 Vancouver riots, at least at the time of writing, there has not been any official RJ intervention. In fact, there have only been three sentencing hearings so far[24] as the criminal justice system is being criticised for its long, cumbersome and expensive process of collecting evidence, identifying offenders and bringing them to justice.

These are some of the reasons that brought together several community leaders, affected businesses, researchers and policy makers to debate whether the available tools are fit for purpose. This meeting was not restorative in nature as it aimed to discuss the potential of RJ in resolving the harm caused to communities post the riots. It was initiated by the Vancouver Association of Restorative Justice (VARJ)[25] and was supported by the Centre for Restorative Justice at Simon Fraser University.[26] Among the attendees was the President of the Downtown Vancouver Business Improvement Association,[27] Charles Gauthier. The local press reported this event as "Shops trashed by rioters consider restorative justice".[28] Gauthier noted: "There is a criminal justice component that we all want to see happen. But there is also the emotional residue from the riot that I think is going to take a little bit longer to find solutions to and bring closure to".[29]

Follow up interviews with experts who were involved in these talks indicated that despite victims' willingness to meet with offenders, VARJ and other RJ organisations are faced with two key challenges when applying RJ for the summer events. The first involves identifying and working with offender rioters. One interviewee noted: "We are all shocked by how slowly the criminal justice system is responding to the riots. In addition to the costs and injustice that this delay causes, it also presents a challenge for RJ practitioners and victims who want to work with these offenders". Someone else said: "If RJ is to be offered post-conviction and as a complementary process, then how can we progress if the justice system is not doing its bit?"

The second challenge relates to funding. Despite the considerable amount spent on criminal investigations, very limited resources are being allocated for practices such as RJ. However, this did not prevent many practitioners and organisation in coming together and acting on a voluntary basis. Although their work did not involve direct RJ encounters it has brought people together to discuss and lobby for better solutions. One research participant said: "When I reflect on the hours of meetings with so many stakeholders over the past 10 months, the amount of volunteer hours that VARJ board members and associates have spent on building capacity for a RJ response in Vancouver, it is staggering". A representative of the Vancouver business community who was interviewed for the study noted: "We would be interested to meet with those who vandalised our businesses. We want to know why they did it, and that they will not do it again". The interviewee continued: "We would not dismiss the idea of supporting financially an RJ initiative".

One example that was carried out on a voluntary basis and was based on the RJ principles involved a circle that was organised at the local church two weeks after the June riots.[30] In consultation with the neighbouring Anglican parish of St. Pauls, the Dean of Christ Church Cathedral convened what he called a *community forum*, open to all, after the Sunday morning liturgy. The Dean said to us: "The purpose of the forum was to provide an opportunity for members of the congregation and others who live in the downtown to share their experiences, thoughts and feelings. I was assisted by a professor of counselling psychology at the University of British Columbia. He facilitated the process and brought with him several graduate students to facilitate the small group circles. About 80 people attended and after introductions, people moved to small groups where they shared their experiences. After their circles, we gathered in a large group and people were invited to come forward and share what they had learned. Some of the highlights from that session included the Roman Catholic priest from the RC Cathedral, who lives right near the epicentre of the riot, speaking of how he offered his church as a place of refuge, and stood out on the street encouraging people to go home. A young man who was at the game and witnessed the riot spoke of his own sense of shame and confusion while the melee was happening around him. A community organizer asked if he could organize a walk from the Cathedral to the site downtown where the worst of the damage of the riot occurred. So, immediately after the forum about 50 of us walked down the streets: we were led by an aboriginal drummer who sang peace songs: with another priest and two politicians I followed the drummer and people followed us. Media covered this ... We stopped and looked at various places ... storefronts still boarded up because windows had been smashed, evidence of burning cars and overturned mailboxes etc. When we got to our destination (Larwill Park) the aboriginal elder offered prayers and sweet grass and I offered a prayer of blessing, praying for the peace of the city and healing for all who had been affected".[31]

It is worth noting that RJ in British Columbia is consistent with the Canadian Criminal Code"[32] (Vancouver Association for Restorative Justice, 2011: 2). In the same paper, the following offer was made: "VARJ has the capacity to bring together respected and highly qualified practitioners and facilitators for a restorative justice project in response to the riot".[33] However, the funding barrier that was identified by two interviewed experts raised questions as to the practicalities of this proposal. "VARJ received very little financial support and despite willingness to provide a cost effective service, this cannot be provided for free" one interviewee said. The second expert was also in agreement.

An interviewee from the provincial Ministry of Justice said: "We would like to work with affected victims, community leaders and practitioners to explore the potential of RJ for the July riots". A representative of the police force, however, expressed strong reservations by saying: "We have a good handle of the situation; identification of all suspects is now almost complete and we have started bringing these criminals to justice. Diverting our energy to implementing untested practices is not wise".

Some of our most powerful data came from a young rioter who in December 2011 was charged for criminal damage that was committed during the July riots. At the time of the interview, he was 20 years old and still waiting to hear about his charges. He said to us, "There isn't a single day that passes by that I don't think in shame about what I did on that day. I wish there was a way to put things right". In a letter he wrote to the Crown counsel and was obtained by our research, he said, "I would love to be able to meet with the owner of the truck that I was photographed in front of. I would like to offer him help if I can. I look forward to somehow righting the wrong done to him and the city of Vancouver that night".

When asked why he got involved in the riots and what led him to join the crowd, he said: "I honestly do not know what happened to me. I can't really explain it. I rarely go downtown – I just went for the game and when I saw lots of people rioting ... well, it looked exciting at the time. I joined and I remember it was as if I was watching myself doing things I would never do". In a letter to the Crown Prosecution, one of his teachers said: "Everyone makes mistakes, whether large or small, publicized or not. I truly believe that X has learned a lot from this experience. It was painful for him, his career has been largely affected and I think I am right in saying that X is no longer the same young person today than a year ago".

An interview with the young rioter's mother helped shed further light on this case. She said to us: "My son has always been hyperactive. At an early stage, he was diagnosed with Attention deficit hyperactivity disorder (ADHD). He engages in sports etc ... This is not an excuse for his involvement. It is just the context. He clearly made some very wrong choices the night of the riot. He felt absolutely devastated about his involvement and has never made any excuses for his actions. He got caught up in the alcohol fuelled mob insanity along with so many other young people that night. X and our family completely understand the anger that surrounds this riot. I felt that same anger watching it on TV that night. Nobody is angrier at X than he is at himself".

In her letter to the Crown Prosecution, the mother wrote, "There was great harm done that night. Not only to property but to the community at large and to the spirit of the city. There certainly needs to be accountability on behalf of the rioters and the needs of the community must be addressed. It seems that the political aim is to punish to the fullest extent of the law". She told us about the shame that her son experienced the next morning. "I had never feared for his safety. I remember driving back home the next morning after talking to him on the phone, fearing that he would do something stupid. He was devastated".

The mother went on, "Is my son any different from many of the young people down there that night? Probably not. I am speaking of a large number of easily excitable, adrenaline fuelled, alcohol induced, impulsive young people who made the mistake of their lives. Are they hard-core criminals? Of course not. Most are likely one-time offenders. Will criminalizing them and/or jailing them help them become criminals? Possibly. Will that be a positive outcome for the community at large? No. Are they likely to be involved in a similar situation again? Not likely. Should they be held accountable and make reparations for their actions? Absolutely! This is where I believe the idea of restorative justice and/or community service comes in. This is not a solution that should be viewed as weak on crime, but rather one that is strong on community. I for one would also be happy to see these kids working with the police – not against them".

Case study no 7: **Greece – ad hoc restorative justice outcome**

Similarly to British Columbia, Greece has not implemented RJ for any of the riot cases that have been prosecuted in relation to the financial crisis. Therefore, our last example is not related to an actual case, but to a restorative outcome that occurred unexpectedly during a public meeting. It refers to the case of journalist Manolis Kypreos which has been widely reported by Greek and international media.[34]

Kypreos was covering the June 2011 riots when he observed abuse of police power by a group of armed officers. Following a discussion with them identifying himself as a journalist, Kypreos was attacked with a stun grenade leaving him deaf and physically disabled. In January 2012, the Athens Public Prosecutor brought charges against unidentified police officers for intentionally causing serious bodily harm. The case was then assigned to a magistrate who is now conducting the investigation. Post the riots, the Police and especially through its collective body, the Hellenic Federation of Police Officers, acknowledged wrong doing by some officers and expressed willingness to review procedures and improve practices. No specific reference or reassurance was given in relation to the Kypreos case.

On 12th October 2011, the Federation organised a meeting to debate the issue of human rights in relation to police powers and riots. Kypreos was invited to give his views. In a private, unpublished recording that was obtained by our research project, Kypreos noted: "I am here to forgive those who left me disabled and ruined my life. I know that at least I can sleep as I have my heart and conscious clear... I also know that police officers are also suffering from the unbearable economic measures ... that you don't have enough to feed your families. I know that you are also losing your homes, just like us journalists and many other citizens. I also know that those who attacked me are the minority. Journalists are on your side exposing truths and encouraging debate. There is nothing that separates us ... Yes, all this time I have been asking the questions "why me". What wrong did I do to them? Why did they target me? I can now reassure you that if this daily death of mine, this torture that I will be suffering until the end of my days, helps to bring us together, then I will say it was worth it and I forgive them".

Immediately after Kypreos' statement, the President of the Federation, Christos Fotopoulous, took the step to publicly apologise for the harm. He added: "I know that apology is not enough. This is why we intend to continue this open dialogue with victims and the community. Hopefully, this will help restore trust". One of the interviewed experts who also happened to be present during this meeting noted: "We were all moved and shocked by the honesty and the sharing that took place during the meeting. It was never intended which is probably why it made it so genuine. It was restorative justice in action only unplanned and ad hoc".

⸱ It is worth noting that RJ in Greece was introduced through the Juvenile Delinquency Law 3189.2003, and domestic violence regulations – Law 3500/2006. Mediation is also provided for civil and commercial matters through Law 3898/2010 and Article 214A of the Greek Code of Civil Procedure (see Gavrielides and Artinopoulou, 2012). Theoretically, RJ is offered at all stages of criminal proceedings through formal and semi-formal practices. However, as the expert interviewee pointed out, "There is lack of statistical data and empirical research on the use of mediation in Greece. There is also lack of appropriate structures and adequate training as well as strong mistrust concerning the effectiveness of RJ schemes. In the absence of a national RJ programme or initiative we are experiencing serious coordination, consistency and quality issues and a strong top down agenda in RJ's implementation".

Chapter Notes

12 Roz Hamilton, GMPT Chief Executive (accessed March 2012) http://www.gm-probation.org.uk/news/default_item.php?id=188

13 Carried out between 7pm- 7am unless work, or significant family responsibilities, would effect this.

14 60-100 hours of Community Payback focused on high visibility task groups working on projects to enhance city / town centre environment.

15 This can only really be done when an offender has admitted what they did was wrong. If they haven't, and still feel what they did was right, it won't have any impact.

16 However, evidence from the IAC that has been running since 2009, and on which the ICRC was based, suggest that 25% of those who were unemployed at the start of their Order obtained employment during the course of their sentence and did not re-offend. The programme also has a successful completion rate of 80%.

17 Following the Public Bodies Reform Bill 2010-11, the new UK government started a process of transferring organisational authority of the YJS from the Youth Justice Board of England and Wales to the Ministry of Justice.

18 The two Acts also introduced Detention and Training Orders, Intensive Supervision and Surveillance Programmes, Bail Supervision and Support programmes, Parenting Orders.

19 (Accessed April 2012) http://www.24dash.com/news/housing/2011-11-17-Young-rioter-apologises-in-face-to-face-meeting-with-victim

20 (Accessed April 2012) http://www.croydon.gov.uk

21 (Accessed April 2012) http://www.thenewlondoners.co.uk/news/395-a-day-in-the-life-elena-noel

22 CARE is a relief and development non-governmental international organization fighting global poverty, see http://www.care-international.org (accessed March 2012).

23 Mahesh Tivedi, "Gujarat Intensifies Drive to Check Falling Sex Ratio". WUNRN www.wunrn.com, April 25, 2007.

24 One received a sentence of 17 months in jail and the other one 40 days http://www.vancouversun.com/news/Vancouver+database+charts+accused+Vancouver+riots/6883947/story.html (Accessed July 2012). The other one pleaded guilty.

25 (Accessed April 2012) http://varjblog.wordpress.com

26 (Accessed April 2012) http://www.sfu.ca/crj

27 (Accessed April 2012) https://netforum.avectra.com/eWeb/StartPage.aspx?Site=DVBIA

28 (Accessed April 2012) http://www.news1130.com/news/local/article/305595--shops-trashed-by-rioters-consider-restorative-justice

29 (Accessed April 2012) http://www.news1130.com/news/local/article/305595--shops-trashed-by-rioters-consider-restorative-justice

30 Various other ad hoc initiatives include rioters' letters of apology to the city of Vancouver, directly to the victim or to the State Prosecutor, see an example (Accessed July 2012) http://www.theprovince.com/news/Stanley+rioter+Robert+Snelgrove+apology+Vancouver/6906454/story.html

31 Further on this can be accessed (April 2012) via http://www.cathedral.vancouver.bc.ca/2011/06/22/vancouver-after-the-riots In September a follow discussion and a play were held at the same location, further (Accessed April 2012) http://www.cathedral.vancouver.bc.ca/event/bascially-good-kids-theatre-forum-september-23-2011

32 Section 718.2(e) states that "all available sanctions other than imprisonment that are reasonable in the circumstances should be considered for all offenders, with particular attention to the circumstances of Aboriginal offenders".

33 http://www.iars.org.uk/sites/default/files/VARJ%20submission%20to%20Vancouver%20Riot%20Review%20of%202011.pdf

34 See for instance (accessed April 2012) http://www.guardian.co.uk/world/2011/nov/27/amnesty-international-50-write-rights

Discussion

From the outset, we have accepted that the purpose of the research was not to paint a statistical picture of RJ with street group violence. Our intention was to drill down into the two notions and understand how they interact with each other, identify key themes and questions that remain unanswered in this grey area of practice, and through the identification of case studies in four countries affected by riots start a debate within policy, academia and practice. Through the context analysis of the collected data, four overarching themes emerged.

"Waves of Healing" model - Piloting evidence-based Restorative Justice with Street Group Violence

In their report for the UK Home Office, Sherman and Strang noted: "The evidence on RJ is far more extensive, and positive, than it has been for many other policies that have been rolled out nationally. RJ is ready to be put to far broader use" (2007: 4). The literature on RJ is extensive and the evidence on its effectiveness and weaknesses with interpersonal crime is rich. Nevertheless, the applicability of RJ with street group violence, as defined by this book, remains a grey area. There is almost no literature on this topic, while the available practice examples are extremely scant. Working with group offenders and their victims may indeed present a new challenge for RJ whose philosophy is based on the principle of mutual understanding, honest and genuine participation and dialogue, empathy and relationship building. Arguably, these are values that gain their meaning at the inter-personal level and not in a group fashion and context.

The various case studies that were discussed in this book suggest that the limited number of street group violence cases that have been tested with RJ practices have been promising. In particular, our analysis of the street group violence phenomenon suggests that its nature presents RJ with a unique opportunity to show its potential. One of the key reasons that led us to this conclusion relates to the significant number of rioters who wake up the next day feeling ashamed for what they did. As suggested by the interviewees of our study, this feeling is rather prominent amongst group offenders due to the dynamics and reasons that encourage the mob mentality that leads to collective harm doing. As one rioter put it: "I was watching myself doing things I would never do ... The next

morning was the worst day of my life. I will never forget the shame I felt ... I still don't know why I joined the crowd".

Furthermore, the overstretched criminal justice system, the rising costs of incarceration and the reduced available resources for the cumbersome, lengthy and costly criminal investigations, make RJ an attractive option for riots. Doubts remain, however, as to the genuine interest in investing in the RJ practice and ethos as this was described in this book. The truth is that once the RJ rhetoric stops and actual practice starts, it becomes apparent that to achieve restorative outcomes, there needs to be enough time, expertise and longevity in the invested project and its processes. This doesn't always sit well with quick fix agendas that want cheaper solutions to complex and new phenomena of violence and crime.

For instance, in the UK, immediately after the summer riots, politicians such as the Mayor of London, Boris Johnson, and the Deputy Prime Minister, Nick Clegg, rushed to pledge their support for RJ-based approaches.[35] However, the evidence shows that despite the many promises, no concrete proposals or indeed practices have been piloted by the top. Even the cases that were identified and sat within the criminal justice system, had a bottom up structure and were initiated by the passion and dedication of practitioners.

On a more positive note, in Canada, efforts that have been made by academics (e.g. Professor Brenda Morrison[36]), practitioners (e.g. Evelyn Zellerer[37]) and pressure groups, such as VARJ, to promote RJ from the bottom up and with rioters are proving fruitful. The provincial Ministry of Justice has just agreed to invest into 20 pilot RJ cases with Vancouver rioters. The outcome of these cases remains to be seen, and the programme of which this book is part of will follow up its findings through observation and qualitative research with them.

There is no doubt that governments across the world are being challenged with criminal justice reforms that aim more for less. While it appears that it is economically advantageous to society to adopt a restorative approach to crime, our research suggests that an appeal solely on this basis may undermine RJ in the long run.

There was consensus among the interviewed practitioners that this could lead to quick fix policies, a lack of a coherent and long-term strategy and high public expectations. For instance, in the UK there has already been criticism of the way cuts are being made in the prison service. For instance, the House of Commons Justice Committee noted: "We have grave concerns about the impact of efficiency savings on practice at the frontline for both prisons and probation, which will undoubtedly undermine the progress in performance of both services. Neither prisons nor probation have the capacity to keep up with the current levels of offenders entering the system. It is not sustainable to finance the costs of running additional prison places and greater probation caseloads from efficiency savings in the long-term" (Justice Committee, 2010: 10).

The fieldwork also raised concerns around the factors that drive social policy and criminal justice reform. For example, the UK interviewees made reference to the government's past commitment for a national strategy on RJ. The discussions were made within a climate of disappointment and suspicion. Specific reference was made to the 2003 Home Office consultation document on the then government's proposed national strategy on RJ. The debate and promises that were made at the time raised the RJ movement's expectations (Gavrielides, 2003). Soon after the publication of the draft strategy, and despite the plethora of evidence it collected through submissions from the public and experts, the flurry of activity and interest in RJ waned. The RJ unit that was set up within the Home Office was dismantled and the majority of the strategy's recommendations were left in draft format. There was no evidence to support this backlash, which was criticised as the outcome of political games and media suspicion (Gavrielides, 2003). It is not surprising why the new Ministry of Justice initiative for a national RJ strategy is seen with suspicion by practitioners.

It is worth nothing that in 2010, the House of Commons Justice Committee said to the then new coalition government, "We are surprised by the cautious approach that the Government has taken towards RJ but we welcome its current commitment to revive the strategic direction in this area. We urge the Justice Secretary to take immediate action to promote the use of RJ and to ensure that he puts in place a fully funded strategy which facilitates national access to RJ for victims before the end of this Parliament" (Justice Committee, 2010: 12). This call is yet to be delivered convincingly by the government.

The trust is that as the world economic downturn is impacting on criminal justice policy and practice and pressure for reform is mounting, the need for an evidence-based approach becomes even more apparent. For the purposes of our research, evidence-based policy and practice is understood as "the integration of the best research evidence with professional expertise and client values in making practice decisions" (McNeese and Thyer, 2004: 8). According to Whyte, evidence-based practice is not one that is driven by populist and political priorities but on that "can be viewed as an attempt at a systematic approach to making decisions that emphasises (a) generating answerable practice questions; (b) locating, critically appraising and interpreting relevant evidence (c) applying best available

evidence in consultation with clients and (d) evaluating the intervention" (2009: 47).

In going forward with RJ and street group violence, concrete pilots will need to be run before any safe claims can be made. Proponents and adversaries of RJ as well as populists and politicians advocating for or against its potential with street group violence will only be able to show their true interest by coming together to pilot the RJ practice. The example of British Columbia is encouraging. Following a presentation of the initial findings of this research,[38] commitment has now been made to invest funding into 20 RJ cases with Vancouver rioters.

Using the findings from the exposed case studies, Table 3 summarises some key ingredients, which based on our research, any RJ pilot with riot cases should include. We call this model "Waves of Healing". The model puts emphasis on building the right infrastructure for restorative practices that can be called for street group violence incidents when and if needed. It assumes that new forms of violence demand new forms of RJ practices. Therefore, it requires a level of innovation and an open mind. These are both characteristics of those working in the voluntary sector as well as of community born practices such as those coming under the banner of RJ. The model moves away from the investment in single practices and organisations, and towards the development of the necessary structures that will allow practitioners (whether in the community or within criminal justice agencies) to respond quickly, effectively and restoratively to further riot related cases.

The list of the elements constructing the proposed model should not be read as restrictive. The model aims to serve as a starting point in constructing what is appropriate for the given pilot. The limitation of our adopted research method as well as the variation in the case studies' location, type of street group violence, timing and extent of their impact should be taken into account.

Table 3: The "Waves of healing" model for restorative justice pilots for street group violence

Key elements	Explanation
Available within and outside of the criminal justice system	There is value in offering RJ for street group violence both through the formal criminal justice system and informally via the community. The latter should not be underestimated given the bottom up nature of RJ, and the need to continue to rely on the passion and voluntary contribution of practitioners.
Exist outside of legislation	Other than case study no 1 and 2 where RJ was clearly provided by law, it is clear that legislation is not a pre-requisite. In fact, in the case of Greece, despite legal provision for mediation no such practice has been promoted from the top down, hierarchical structure of the Hellenic penal system. In the case of British Columbia, despite legislation, RJ was developed voluntarily and in the shadows of the formal criminal justice system.
Available to juveniles and adult group offenders	As there is no evidence to suggest that RJ is not appropriate with adult street group offenders, based on the presented case studies there is no evidence to recommend focusing on a particular age group.
The voluntariness principle	This should be applied religiously and consistently for both the offenders and victims. An extension of this principle is the right to withdraw at any stage of the process. This should not have an impact on the case as it is returned back to the criminal justice system.
Available post-conviction; mostly applicable post sentencing	The limited practice seems to have focused on RJ's implementation as a complementary option that is offered to the riots offenders and victims post-conviction. In some occasions, this was also offered prior sentencing or had an impact on the imposed sentenced.
Involves a multi-staged process of reparation, victim awareness and citizenship in advance of restorative encounter	Like most RJ practice, it should not be expected that an encounter should be made available without appropriate preparation. Especially in the case of street group offenders, intense citizenship and victim awareness sessions were thought to be paramount. Risk assessment and a dialogue that leads to informed choice were key conditions.

Table 3: The "Waves of healing" model for restorative justice pilots for street group violence (continued)

Key elements	Explanation
Restorative outcomes must be central; distinguishing RJ based practices from community payback	The various independent reports that followed the examined riots quoted several examples of community activism such as cleaning the streets and fixing damaged property. Community payback was also praised. To fully enjoy the outcomes of RJ its processes must be engaged. These require an encounter between the offender and the victim. The examined cases included both direct and indirect methods including interventions while the given events were taking place. Emphasis was given in restoring harm than applying rigidly structures that could potentially lead to restorative outcomes.
Meetings with group offenders are possible, but resource intensive	Including more than 3 street group offenders in one RJ encounter proved a challenge particularly due to the intense preparatory time and resource that had to be invested. This also involved additional time and stages that had to be completed in ensuring that the victim did not feel a power imbalance and that the risk of re-victimisation was removed.
Victim-led practices	Where RJ practices are initiated by the victim, they have more chances of being materialised. This also includes the business community as a victim. This is particularly true for street group violence given that in addition to the individual victims the community is always affected as a group entity.
Offenders' resettlement post RJ is paramount	The case studies stressed the importance of providing follow up integration and resettlement services to the street group offenders who had undergone RJ. Mentoring, employment, training and psychological support were all mentioned.
Multi-agency, cross sector partnership delivery model	Engaging RJ for street group violence requires a combination of expertise and the ability to reach into communities. Driving this practice by a single agency proved difficult. Where multi-agency, cross-sector partnerships were formed between community-based practitioners, criminal justice agencies, health and social support workers, the challenges were less prominent.
Continuity; adequate resourcing	Lack of commitment for adequate resourcing also meant lack of continuity and reduced impact. Building community relations and offering a chance to large numbers of street group offenders to repair requires long term processes and investment.
Restoration of feelings and finances	Restoring feelings was considered as significant as restoring the economic impact of street group violence. Where assault and other forms of physical violence had occurred, this was not as prominent. However, for practices initiated by business-victims, financial restoration was paramount.

The restorative justice ethos:
Under the radar of research and evaluation

Related to the above is the controversy on what constitutes robust evaluation of the RJ ethos and practices. Our research suggested that there is a tension between officials and researchers on what constitutes evidence. As Bryman (2004) points out, the gold standard is usually thought to be quantitative data from randomised controlled trials. This is particularly true for civil servants who are quick to dismiss credible and in-depth new knowledge simply because it is not based on large units (e.g. see Gavrielides, 2011b).

As the rich RJ literature suggests, when it comes to complex notions such as RJ and how it interacts with offenders and victims, "the abstraction inherent in quantitative studies" hinders the process of understanding (Miles and Huberman, 1994: 41). As Bryman puts it, qualitative research allows for "an inductive theorizing about the way individuals (the sample) interpret their social worlds" (2004: 63). The same applies to sampling strategies. Bryman's warning is brought to mind as he alerts us not to be consumed by stringent methodological sampling rules. The qualitative type of research strategy, he said, is not meant to be based on comparisons of variables, but on substantive, in-depth qualitative discussions among participants (2004).

Furthermore, there is also a tension between researchers and RJ practitioners. As noted in Gavrielides, "There is consensus in the literature that there is still a long way to go before the RJ movement can safely claim that its practitioners, researchers and policy makers are all moving in the same direction" (2011b: 4). Gavrielides (ibid) noted that a number of RJ practitioners see researchers 'feeding' on their case-work and then dictating how they should do their work. A practitioner interviewed for our study noted, "There is an imbalance that urgently needs to be addressed. Research should be carried out only into those areas which support original hypothesis. Conversely, practices which haven't been properly researched should be condemned by policy makers and funders". The same practitioners warned against arriving at a state of orthodoxy which threatens the growth of knowledge.

Gavrielides also noted: "There was a consensus [by the research participants] that there is a need for practitioners to publish and promote their work and be involved in teaching and supervision. Research in partnership needs to be pushed even further and indeed encouraged by government. It was agreed that there is a need to bring together practitioners and agencies and that more networking within the field was needed" (2011b: 6).[39]

In going forward, any future RJ pilot with street group violence will need to include in-built evaluation. A good and solid partnership between researchers, practitioners and policy makers will need to be achieved. This will require an acceptance of the RJ principles. Too often RJ evaluation is hampered due to the focus it has been given by criminal justice agencies.

The truth is that evaluation has traditionally been associated with the question of 'what works', and therefore it generally aims to prove or disprove the predefined targets of the given organisation that is funding it (let that be public or private). However, this question is relative and to a great extent misleading, as it can involve virtually anything in the appropriate conditions. That is why many researchers like Marshall and Merry have insisted that "the approach should change from 'what works' to 'what exactly happened' (in certain specific instances)" (1990: 20).

As a rule of thumb, evaluators should not be concerned with the policy decision that will eventually follow their work on whether to continue with the given programme or action. This is primarily a political decision that involves a number of moral and ideological factors that the researcher may attempt to clarify but cannot decide. That is why a good evaluator focuses on collecting information relevant to all the identifiable aims, which different parties may have. Especially in the case of RJ with riots, researchers need to include all its targeted audiences: victims, offenders and communities, and disengage with media driven agendas.

Due to the politically charged nature of street group violence, this danger is exacerbated. Often evaluators are supplied with predefined tasks that are set out to be proved or disproved, having to move within the retributivist and utilitarian understanding of the given funding bodies. These tasks usually involve the reduction of re-offending, saving police time, the reduction of costs and the prison population. This narrows the scope of the evaluation and its chances of reflecting practical reality.

The challenge posed by this problem is one of foremost significance for RJ's future development for street group violence. It is also one of the most difficult to address, since it requires a certain level of transformation of the culture that is currently inherent in criminal justice policy agendas. It does not relate to a specific political party. A change in culture demands a slow and long process. It also needs to persuade funders and policymakers about the usefulness and significance of these 'other' targets that are set by RJ. If practitioners and researchers can show that through their completion, these targets may lead to an outcome that is fairer, more efficient, less time-consuming and more cost-effective than the one pursued through punitive targets set up by the traditional criminal justice system, then this pitfall might be overcome.

One of the most consistent findings from the fieldwork highlighted the need for maintaining the ethos and values of RJ. There was concern that principles are being watered down to fit in with funding restrictions and pre-fixed priorities. As one practitioner commented: "So, when you get money from the Government, then it is likely that you get their agenda, and this affects how to measure the value of RJ and its outcomes". The interviewees pointed out that to justify their existence and funding, RJ practices in the secure estate have to appeal to the persuasive power of utilitarian or economic rationalism. This means that they have to show that: (a) they will decrease court caseloads, the prisoner population, and recidivism rates; and (b) they will increase the percentage of restitution settlements and victim/offender satisfaction.

According to the interviewees, it is likely that if RJ projects and their evaluation continue to be funded according to the aforementioned two criteria, then its original values and principles will be skewed and possibly merged with the retributive and utilitarian objectives of the traditional criminal justice system. The sample seemed to believe that the predominance of retributive goals in the criminal justice system in combination with the secondary role that has been bestowed on restorative practices expose the concept to a 'no-win' process, where restorative ideals are called to compete with the already deep-rooted beliefs of 'law and order' to which most policymakers and politicians adhere.

However, focusing solely on the targets and outcomes of a restorative programme cannot be enough in bringing a change to the aforementioned culture. In fact, and this is where the heart of the problem lies, evaluation needs to embrace a range of other factors apart from programmes' *outcomes*. The RISE experiments in Australia (Sherman et al, 2000) have set an example, while the following variants need to be considered at all times:

- **Participant satisfaction**: In mediation this should refer to both victims and offenders. In conferencing, circles and boards, this could also extend to secondary and tertiary participants. Satisfaction, on the other hand, should be measured not only in terms of the process in the narrow sense, but also in terms of the whole restorative experience (e.g. overall satisfaction with the facilitator, the preparation, the venue, timing, procedural features *strictu sensu*, etc.). It could also include questions such as recommending the process to others or choosing to participate again.
- **'Restorativeness' of the process**: Undoubtedly, this factor will constitute one of the greatest challenges for future evaluation particularly since its

measurement will require a certain level of agreement around the essential restorative values. These could include, for example, expressions of feelings, genuine remorse and asking/giving of apology, consensus and understanding, honest and productive dialogue, sense and willingness of reintegration.

- **Restorative Outcomes**: These need not only be the ability of the programme to reduce re-offending and save police time or financial resources, but could include the effects on victims and offenders and their families. For example, reduced anger and fear, improved quality of life, benefits to the community and restoration of businesses.

- **Delivery**: This could just focus on the ability and competence of facilitators to carry out meetings according to the generally accepted restorative values and the nationally established training standards. The establishment of the accreditation procedure and committee as well as the introduction of nationally accepted manuals, books, standards and other quality criteria that have been suggested in other parts of the book will assist in this measurement.

On the other hand, the evaluators themselves also carry an enormous amount of responsibility in this long-term process of cultural transformation. Most often, while in theory the measurement of outcomes is important to evaluation, in practice this significance is over stressed; "In the struggle for shares in limited budgets, advocates of particular innovations are liable to be forced into claiming more for their ideas than in the face of other inimical social forces can be attained" (Marshall and Merry, 1990: 24).

Finally, evaluation has so far focused only on individual-level outcomes or types of programmes. More importantly, it has used measures and techniques that are typical in the measurement of traditional criminal justice procedures (see King et al, 2008). The need to develop more innovative measures that would allow for the evaluation of a more wide-ranging RJ and more accurate data on the quality and effectiveness of its outcomes and procedures is therefore identified.

It is important that future research reflects both the *outcomes* of the evaluated programmes as well as those features that quantify what Braithwaite has called "grace, shalom" (2002b: 53). While taking care that the right balance between these two targets is achieved, evaluators need also to make sure that a distinction is made between the *ultimate* objectives of the process and its *intermediate* outcomes. As Marshall and Merry put it: "Almost any scheme associated with criminal justice will invite the majority of observers to identify the reduction of crime as the prime aim. The dominance of this criterion has probably led to the demise of many promising ideas" (1990: 30).

These 'other' objectives of restorative practices need to address at least two needs. First, they need to show to the given parties that the process is indeed worthwhile and effective. Therefore, they have to meet the needs and expectations of the primary participants. Second, if RJ is to be accepted as a social policy it has to show that in its new ultimate objectives there are benefits not only for the individual participants, but also for the wider social and economic circles. There must also be a feeling that "the provision of such services is obligatory upon society" (Marshall and Merry, 1990: 31).

Public Perception & Victims' Support

There is a general assumption that victims and the public reject the idea of RJ (e.g. see De Mesmaecker, 2010; Gavrielides, 2007). However, the evidence shows that victims are not as punitive as thought by politicians and policy makers (e.g. see Sherman and Strang, 2007). Even in sensitive cases such as hate crime (Gavrielides 2011c; 2012b) and sexual abuse (Gavrielides and Coker 2005; Pelikan, 2012; Gavrielides 2012c) where a power relationship is preceded, victims' willingness to engage in a direct or indirect encounter exceeds 80%.

In the case of street group violence, following the England riots, an ICM poll that was conducted in September 2011 on behalf of Prison Reform Trust showed that 88% of the 1000 people who were interviewed thought victims of theft and vandalism should be given the chance to let offenders know of the harm and distress they have caused. The idea of RJ was backed by 94% . Furthermore, almost three quarters (71%) believed victims should have a say in how the offender can best make amends for the harm they have caused. Lower income groups, who are more likely to be victims of crime, were most in favour of adopting community payback and a restorative justice approach. Interestingly, fewer than two thirds (65%) believed that a prison sentence would be effective. One in four felt expressly that it would not be effective in preventing crime and disorder (ICM, 2011).

In the case of Vancouver, an online poll taken in December 2011 by News1130 showed that the majority of survey respondents (58%) approved of RJ as response to the summer riots.[44] Moreover, in their report "Let's Talk about it", The Vancouver District Student Council, stated their overwhelming support for RJ.[45] The Vancouver business community also expressed its support in exploring the potential of RJ for its victim-business members.[46] A representative of the

Chart 1: What the public wants: Riots & Restorative justice (ICM poll, England 2011)

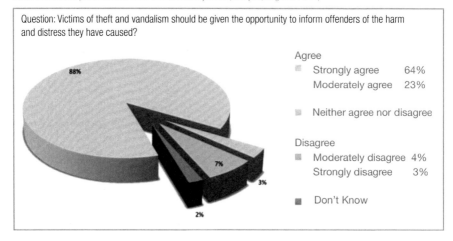

Question: Victims of theft and vandalism should be given the opportunity to inform offenders of the harm and distress they have caused?

88%

7%

3%

2%

Agree
- Strongly agree 64%
  Moderately agree 23%

- Neither agree nor disagree

Disagree
- Moderately disagree 4%
  Strongly disagree 3%

- Don't Know

Vancouver business community said in one of our interviews, "We would be keen to explore the potential of RJ with those who damaged our businesses. Provided that we can always return to the justice system should RJ fail, then I do not see a reason why business owners should not meet with the rioters who vandalised their properties". The research findings of Shankar and Gerstein (2007) for the Gujarat riots and the views of victims have already been discussed in this book, while no survey has been conducted in relation to the Greek riots.

One interviewee from the UK said: "I have met young people who simply want to speak to the shop owners, to give them their property back and to have them forgive them. They did it in the heat of the moment. How much money do we have to spend in catching them, punishing them when these shop owners may in the end never get their property back? They want to come forth; they want dialogue".

Innovative Justice through user-led evidence

There is no doubt that RJ is back on the agenda. The reasons that sparked this interest vary. The increasing number of suicides by young prisoners, the overcrowded prisons and the inhumane conditions to which young people and children are subjected, the high rates of reoffending and the rising costs of incapacitation as a policy and a philosophy for crime control are some of the factors that populists quote in their search for innovative solutions (Gavrielides, 2012a). Since most governments are determined to cut down their national deficits by any means possible, this presents a unique opportunity to rethink existing strategies within the criminal justice system.

The message from governments, the media, and academia is that further spending on imprisonment is not intended or indeed considered to be the right way forward at present. Baxter et al said: "Continued budgetary pressure and associated austerity measures are forcing a rethink of how justice services are delivered. Police forces, courts, probation trusts, prisons and community organisations must continually reduce their spending in the coming years. In this environment, innovation can and should play a major role in driving efficiency, meeting cost targets and developing new and better ways of delivering justice services" (2011: 4).

In addition to these challenges, the policy and political community is also called to respond to new trends of anti-social behaviour, one of which is riots. Moving quickly, flexibly and innovatively within the civil service and public sector service provision is not easy hence the increased attention that has been given to community-based criminal justice services including mediation, circles and conferencing. Despite its deep historical roots (e.g. see Gavrielides and Winterdyk, 2011; Gavrielides, 2011d), RJ is still viewed as a "new" and innovative approach to social and criminal deviance (e.g. see Walgrave, 2012).

Claims that RJ is a cheaper option must be balanced against the scant available data. Looking at the basic economic theory model, it uses the price (cost) of a commodity or how service affects the relationships or quantity of that commodity that people (service users) would wish to purchase at each price. Put another way, for every price, a certain quantity will be demanded, and likewise, for every price, a certain quantity will be supplied. Therefore, it is assumed that the higher the price, the less will be demanded, and the higher the price, the more will be supplied.

In the case of RJ, the scarce evidence suggests that the savings that flow from the contribution made by RJ to reducing reoffending rates are positive. On the other hand, we know that crime by former prisoners costs society more than £11 billion per year (Prison Reform Working Group, 2009), while RJ can deliver cost savings of up to £9 for every £1 spent (Shapland et al., 2008). According to Victim Support (2010: 29), "if RJ were offered to all victims of burglary, robbery and violence against the person where the offender had pleaded guilty (which would amount to around 75,000 victims), the cost savings to the criminal justice system - as a result of a reduction in reconviction rates - would amount to at least £185 million over two years".

In going forward, RJ has to convince on two fronts. First, it must show that it provides better justice for the parties involved; this will need to be cheaper and more adaptive to the needs and current realities of our times. Second, that while doing so, it places public protection at the heart of its practices. High profile cases highlighting failures, the exposition of victims and communities to re-victimisation, will quickly result in investment decrease.

Many have argued that to construct successful and innovate criminal justice policies and practices, the user must be involved (Cass, 2010; Crawford and Rutter, 2004; Baxter et al, 2011; Gavrielides, 2012d). For our research purposes, the term "user" is understood to include the offender, the victim and their communities. Baxter et al. noted, "Breakthrough improvements are possible by taking innovative approaches, in particular by engaging offenders, communities and the private sector in new forms of service delivery: new processes, new services and new business models" (2011: 4). It is doubtful how much user involvement currently takes place in the formation of criminal justice policy and practice. The case studies clearly suggest that when a practice is victim initiated there are more chances of completing it. The available research data also suggests that user-led (e.g. victim-led) RJ programmes tend to have higher rates of success and better outcomes for all. Gavrielides (2012d) argues that a true participatory democracy is only one that allows and indeed enables users and citizens, independently of their circumstances, to have a choice in the decision making structures that affect their lives.

Additional barriers that were mentioned by the interviewees as hindering the process of innovation within RJ were "organisational silo structures" and the reluctance to deviate from top down performance targets which most of the times are linked with Treasury funding. One interviewee said: "There is a strong culture of risk aversion within public sector justice services. We have to fight with this every time we propose something that is not seen as a priority or indeed as a potential risk to what is considered a norm". Another barrier that was mentioned is the lack of effective leadership from managers and politicians. While frontline staff in police, prosecution and probation may be willing to adapt current practice to respond to innovative and cost effective RJ methodologies, they are often challenged by their managers who remain focused on delivering organisational strategies. Baxter et al. (2011) also agree with this finding as they point out that managerial support will need to be strong not only from the start but also during development and implementation; "During development, leaders play a key role in defining how new ideas relate to existing performance measures and governance structures. During implementation, sponsorship and continued support of the project team is critical" (Baxter *et al.*, 2011: 4).

The truth is that the extant literature does not reflect the breadth of innovation and indeed the various practice models that come under the banner of RJ. For instance, many have tried to "map" RJ practices within the prison setting (e.g. see Liebmann, 2004; Dhami et al., 2009; Gavrielides, 2012a) but due to their continuously evolving nature and the lack of any systematic and consistent application, these "maps" become very quickly obsolete and inaccurate. Statutory services have to rely on voluntary and community groups to publicise, disseminate and share best practices. At the same time, the research community needs to adapt its approach and welcome models of evaluation that are inclusive of such practices.

Knowledge about the voluntary sector's role in crime control is principally based on anecdotal evidence and only rarely are scientific studies published on its contribution and evaluation. The infrastructure for developing such knowledge is absent while academia itself needs to develop its thinking even further in the development of clearer goals of research for RJ. If the RJ rhetoric is to be taken forward, researchers should not just focus on matters of immediate policy and practical relevance. Instead, a broader academic agenda is proposed. Distance will need to be taken between the goals of RJ and the goals of academic research.

As expressed in other works, one of the biggest strengths of RJ is the passion and commitment that exists among mediators and RJ practitioners (Gavrielides, 2007). Meanwhile, Braithwaite (2002b) warned that if this passion is tampered with, there is real danger that RJ may lose its authenticity. The study continues to be sceptical about top down approaches that attempt to define the future of RJ in the UK. The study also remains dubious about the reasons that drive current legislative and institutional proposals for a change in the philosophy and practice of sentencing and crime control.

Chapter Notes

35 For Johnson see http://www.guardian.co.uk/politics/davehillblog/2011/aug/15/boris-johnson-seeks-restorative-justice-for-london-rioters (accessed April 2012). For Clegg see http://www.restorative justice.org.uk/news/nick_clegg_announces_plans_for_restorative_justice_in_response_to_the_riots (Accessed April 2012)
36 Centre for Restorative Justice, Simon Fraser University http://www.sfu.ca/crj (Accessed July 2012)
37 Peace of the Circle, http://www.peaceofthecircle.com (accessed July 2012)
38 Following an invitation by the Centre for Dialogue at Simon Fraser University, Gavrielides presented initial findings at the Bruce and Lis Welch Community Dialogue in Vancouver. For a summary of the media

coverage and the activities relating to this event http://www.iars.org.uk/content/RJ_Riots_IARS2012 (Accessed July 2012) Gavrielides' presentation for the Welch community Award on restorative justice and riots can be downloaded from http://www.iars.org.uk/sites/default/files/RJ%20IARS%2018%201% 2012.ppt (accessed July 2012). The lecture can viewed from http://www.youtube.com/watch?v=nPHP JsK6LmY&feature=relmfu (Accessed July 2012).

39 This conclusion is also supported by Dally, 2003 and Gavrielides, 2007.

40 See for instance, recent misreporting of RJ http://www.bbc.co.uk/news/uk-england-leeds-15870279

41 This included a random sample of 1,000 adults aged 18+ on a Telephone Omnibus between 2 and 4 September. Surveys were conducted across England, and the results were weighted to the profile of all adults. ICM is a member of the British Polling Council.

42 (Accessed April 2012) http://www.prisonreformtrust.org.uk

43 (Accessed April 2012) http://www.prisonreformtrust.org.uk/PressPolicy/News/ItemId/143/vw/1

44 (Accessed April 2012) http://www.news1130.com/news/local/article/305595--shops-trashed-by -rioters-consider-restorative-justice

45 (Accessed April 2012) http://vdsc.ca/wp-content/uploads/2011/07/VDSC-Lets-Talk-About-It-Official -Report-pdf.pdf

46 See statement by the Downtown Vancouver Business Improvement Association President Charles Gauthier (accessed April 2012) http://www.news1130.com/news/local/article/305595--shops-trashed-by-rioters -consider-restorative-justice

Concluding Thoughts

The arguments and findings of this book were developed in a climate that favours RJ. This has not always been the case for the RJ movement. The current world economic crisis, the overburdened criminal justice system, the rising costs of imprisonment and claims that RJ can increase victim satisfaction and reduce recidivism bring restorative practices to the forth of political discussions worldwide. We approached this increasing interest with suspicion.

We also tried to view RJ from a balanced point of view although the initial hypothesis that our research aimed to test placed RJ within a criminological field that is considered a new territory for its practices. Undoubtedly, over the last two decades, the literature and research on RJ have grown to an impressive standard. In fact, RJ appears to be backed up by more evidence than many other criminal justice policies that are often picked up as quick fix solutions to new trends of anti-social behaviour. This research aimed to challenge RJ by looking at its potential outside of its comfort zone of interpersonal crimes. The growing phenomenon of street group violence may indeed present restorativists with fresh ground for practice and research. When do group offending dynamics take over and overpower individual control? Or is the group dynamic just an opportunity to allow our basic instincts to have free play, and therefore worthy of harsher punishment? When does individual responsibility begin and end? How can RJ be appropriate for these cases, if its very ethos and the success of its practices lie in the taking up of individual responsibility?

The recent riots in the examined four countries gave us the backdrop of this investigation, which remains incomplete. From the outset, we accepted that our case study method and findings were not meant to serve as universal truths but as stimuli for further investigation within academia, policy and practice. We also hope that this book has opened up the debate on RJ's appropriateness with group violence that occurs on the streets.

We have found a fantastic rhetoric about the potential of RJ with riots. This is being developed by well-intended practitioners and politicians. The reality is that there is only a handful of RJ cases with riots. This is due to a combination of factors, such as the lack of available data on RJ's effectiveness, the absence of funding and the right infrastructure and expertise to implement RJ. But how about the rioters themselves? And victims? What do they want? And what does the community really need to heal? Our approach to developing RJ further must remain evidence-based. This book merely scratches the surface of a complicated issue and a grey area of practice – more evidence is needed from affected parties and the community.

As a way forward, it was recommended that pilots are developed for testing RJ with street group violence. Our analysis constructed a conceptual framework within which these pilots can be placed, and asked for in-built evaluation that looks both at processes and outcomes. In Vancouver, as a result of our project and the intervention of a number of stakeholders, these pilots are now underway. This research represents only the first step in understanding RJ's potential with street group violence. The larger programme within which this book is placed will continue its investigation while more international partnerships and cases are pursued.

Our study has warned that to avoid disappointment, policy makers and practitioners must remain focused on achieving RJ's true intentions and safeguarding its ethos. These are often skewed by other criminal justice priorities. The introduction of this report also stressed the importance of adopting a definition for RJ that is centered in its values and not so much in its processes. Accepting that RJ is an ethos with practical goals opens up its potential with street group violence.

In fact, our research suggested that we may have to think in a completely different way if we are to apply RJ in the context of street group violence. It follows from our model that there is a need to have an existing structure and infrastructure that come live as soon as an event takes place; mediators moving into a riot would be one such example. As a new model, we could measure needs of victims and quantify any loss and the needs for recovery. The people with the brooms, cleaning the streets after the riots, are the live example of community will that draws together all affected parties to restore the collective harm that street group violence causes.

We concluded that if a riot does not fit the model of face-to-face, inter-personal crime, and it is indeed too big and unstructured, then the restorative response will not fit a rigidly structured RJ process, such as a scripted conference. We know that most of the case studies that were cited in our research could easily be rejected by RJ purists who accept only interventions that interfere with the criminal justice system process either through sentencing or prosecution. Although RJ's contribution to relieving the formal justice system is welcomed, it is not one of its central intentions. As argued, the RJ ethos is centered in restoring harm independently of whether this is interpreted to be "criminal" and prosecutable. The Greek case study is a good example of how restoration and healing can be achieved without interfering with formal structures. On the other hand, it is one thing carrying out good community gestures of restoration, such as cleaning the streets and marching, and another pursuing justice that diverts cases from the formal criminal justice system. Our research suggests that in the case of street group violence, what we may indeed need is layer upon layer of restorative input. We have come to call this "waves of healing".

As we wait for this research to follow up its findings through evaluation of actual RJ interventions with riot cases, we point out that fresh thinking around what makes it successful in the context of street group offending is warranted. We already knew that as a community born practice, RJ, and any new attempt to develop it, must be grounded in the experiences of its users and practitioners. Top down approaches that aim to mainstream it are bound to fail despite their good intentions. In the case of street group violence, the role of the community in initiating, driving and monitoring RJ's implementation is even more significant. Multiple offenders mean multiple victims, and multiple victims often mean community.

Our study also identified an additional role for communities, other than initiating and driving the restorative practice. This involves the development of social policy through the collection of user-led evidence. Innovative justice is now considered the main way forward in dealing with persistent criminality and the rising costs of traditional criminal justice approaches. But without the genuine involvement of the user and investment in communities, innovation will remain an empty concept packed with data and theories that are removed from our realities.

To conclude, politicians, victims and practitioners have to ask themselves what are they really trying to achieve by bringing RJ to the table of the recent riot discussions. If the intentions are merely to cut down costs and appear modern and innovative, then the proposed pilots will prove to be a waste of time. If the focus is on restorative outcomes and the true empowerment of communities, then innovation will be found. We have shown that the community sector and multi-agency partnerships can help bring healing to communities and group victims who will continue to be affected by the growing phenomenon of street group violence.

This proposition is not normative in nature. On the contrary, prioritising RJ outcomes with an emphasis on communities will help make the RJ notion more concrete and real. Much of the rhetoric that quickly developed around RJ and riots has been damaging for the movement. It promotes a fictitious RJ concept. This has to stop.

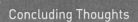

Using the example of rights and duties, John Stuart Mill helps us to understand that if we merely base our thinking and practice on constructs without consequences, then much energy will be wasted. RJ can gain significance only in so far as it can be paraphrased into sentences explaining what the ultimate outcome of its processes will be. That outcome is the "real entity" that should drive our pilots and its evaluation and research. Without this RJ will remain, what Mill calls, a "fictitious entity". He said: "If the fictitious entities we use cannot be so translated, then they have no real meaning and operate as confusions and mysteries behind which sinister interests operate to their own advantage" (Mill, 1993: 11).

Bibliography

Ahmed, S. (2004). "Sustaining Peace, Re-Building Livelihoods: The Gujarat Harmony Project". Vol 12: 3 *Gender and Development*, pp. 94-102.

Allport, G.W (1954). *The Nature of Prejudice*. Cambridge: Addison-Wesley.

Anderson, E. (1999). Code of the Street: Decency, Violence, and the Moral Life of the Inner City. New York: W. W. Norton.

Baxter, D et al (2011). *Innovation in Justice: New Delivery Models and Better Outcomes*, Bedfordshire: Cranfield University.

Bazemore, G. & L. Walgrave (1998). *Restorative Juvenile Justice: Repairing the Harm of Youth Crime*, Monsey, NY USA: Criminal Justice Press.

Bigelow, R. (1969). *The dawn warriors*. Boston: Little-Brown.

Braithwaite, J. (2002a). "Setting Standards for Restorative Justice", *British Journal of Criminology*, 42, pp. 563-577.

Braithwaite, J. (2002b) *Restorative Justice & Responsive Regulation*, Oxford: Oxford University Press.

Bryman, A. (2004). *Social Research Methods*. Oxford: Oxford University Press.

Cass, R. (2010). "Creating space for young people's voices; an investigation into the youth-led approach". *Youth Voice Journal,* 1:1, 4-16.

Christie, N. (1977). 'Conflicts as Property', *British Journal of Criminology* 17(1), 1-15.

Clark, J.N. (2008) "The three Rs: retributive justice, restorative justice, and reconciliation", *Contemporary Justice Review* Vol. 11, No. 4, pp. 331–350.

Crawford, A. and Newburn, T. (2003) *Youth Offending and Restorative Justice: Implementing Reform in Youth Justice*, Cullompton, Devon: Willan Pub.

Crawford, M.J. and Rutter, D. (2004) "Are the views of members of mental health user groups representative of those of 'ordinary' patients? A cross-sectional survey of service users and providers". *Journal of Mental Health*, 13(6), 561–568.

Daly, Kathleen (2003).Mind the Gap: Restorative Justice in Theory and Practice in, Andrew von Hirsch, *et. al.*, eds., *Restorative Justice and Criminal Justice: Competing or Reconcilable Paradigms?* Oxford and Portland, Orgeon: Hart Publishing. Pp. 219-236.

De la Rey, C. (2001). "Reconciliation in Divided Societies". In D.J. Christie, R.V Wagner and D. D. Winter (Eds.), *Peace, Conflict and Violence: Peace Psychology for the 21st Century*, Upper Saddle River: Prentice Hall, pp. 251-261.

De la Roche, R. (1996). "Collective violence as Social Control", *Sociological Forum*, Vol. 11: 1, pp. 97-128.

De Mesmaecker, V. (2010). "Building social support for restorative justice through the media: is taking the victim perspective the most appropriate strategy?", *Contemporary Justice Review*, Vol. 13, No. 3, pp. 239–267.

Dhami, M.K., G. Mantle,and Fox, D. (2009). "Restorative justice in prisons", *Contemporary Justice Review*, 12: 4, 433 — 448.

Dicklitch, S. and A. Malik (2010). Justice, Human Rights, and Reconciliation in Postconflict Cambodia, *Hum Rights Review* 11, pp. 515–530.

Durrant, R. (2011). "Collective violence: An evolutionary perspective", *Aggression and Violent Behavior*, 16, pp. 428–436.

Eisenhardt, K. M. (1989). Building theories from case study research. Academy of Management Review, 14(4), 352-550.

Eglash, A. (1977) 'Beyond Restitution: Creative Restitution', in J. Hudson and B. Galaway (eds) *Restitution in Criminal Justice*, pp. 91–129. Lexington, MA: DC Heath & Company.

Fogelson, R. (1970). "Violence and Grievances: Reflections on the 1960s riots", *Journal of Social Issues*, 26, pp. 141-163.

Furlong, J. and D. Keefe (2011). *The Night the City Became a Stadium*. Vancouver.

Gat, A. (2006). *War in human civilization*. Oxford: Oxford University Press.

Gavrielides, T. and V. Artinopoulou (2012). "Violence against women and restorative justice", Asian Journal of Criminology, ISNN 1871-0131.

Gavrielides, T. (2012a) *Rights and Restoration within youth justice*, de Sitter Publications: Canada.

Gavrielides, T. (2012b). "Contextualising Restorative Justice for Hate Crime". *Journal of Interpersonal Violence*.

Gavrielides, T. (2012c). " Clergy Child Sexual Abuse & the Restorative Justice Dialogue", *Journal of Church and State*.

Gavrielides, T. (2012d). "User-led Youth Justice Policy: a Participatory Democracy through Restorative Justice and Human Rights" in Gavrielides, T. (eds). *Rights and Restoration Within Youth Justice*, Whitby, ON: de Sitter Publications.

Gavrielides, T. (2011a). *Restorative Justice and the Secure Estate: Alternatives for Young People*, London: IARS.

Gavrielides, T. (2011b) Drawing together research, policy and practice for restorative justice, London: IARS.

Gavrielides, T. (2011c). "Restorative Practices & Hate Crime: Opening up the debate". 14:4 Temida, 7-19

Gavrielides, T. (2011d). "Restorative Practices: From the Early Societies to the 1970s". *Internet Journal of Criminology* ISSN 2045-6743 (Online).

Gavrielides, T. (2008) "Restorative justice: the perplexing concept. Conceptual fault lines and power battles within the restorative justice movement" 8:2 *Criminology and Criminal Justice Journal*, 165-183.

Gavrielides, T. (2007) *Restorative Justice Theory and Practice: Addressing the Discrepancy*, HEUNI: Helsinki.

Gavrielides, T. (2003) "Restorative Justice: Are we there yet? Responding to the Home Office's Consultation Questions", 14:4 *Criminal Law Forum*, pp. 385-419.

Gavrielides, T. and J. Winterdyk (2011). "The fall and rise of restorative justice: a historical account of its notion, practices and possible lessons learned", Vol 2 & 3, *Pakistan Journal of Criminology*, pp. 107-125.

Gavrielides T. and D. Coker (2005) "Restoring Faith: Resolving the Catholic Church's Sexual Scandals through Restorative Justice: Working Paper I", 8:4 *Contemporary Justice Review*, pp. 345-365.

Hamel, J. (1993). Case study methods. Newbury Park, CA: Sage.

Harsh, M. (2004). *Cry, My Beloved Country: Reflections on the Gujarat Carnage*, Delhi: Rainbow Publishers.

Harsh, M. (2003). "Compounding Injustice: the Government's failure to redress massacres in Gujarat", 15:3 *India*, 4.

Helie, A. *et al* (2003). *Threatened Existence: A Feminist analysis of the genocide in Gujarat*. Bombay: New Age Printing Press.

Home Office (1998). *No More Excuses-A New Approach to Tackling Youth Crime in England and Wales*, London: HMSO.

ICM (2011). *Theft and Vandalism Survey: CATI Fieldwork 2-4 September 2011*, London: ICM.

Johnstone, G. and D.V, Ness (2011). *Handbook of Restorative Justice*, Cullompton: Willan publishing.

Justice Committee (2010). *Cutting crime: the case for justice reinvestment*, London: House of Commons.

Kelly, R. C. (2000). *Warless societies and the origin of war*. Ann Arbor, MI: The University of Michigan Press.

King, R. et al (2008). *Doing Research on Crime and Justice*, Oxford: Oxford University Press.

Kohen, A., M. Zanchelli and L. Drake (2011). "Personal and Political Reconciliation in Post-Genocide Rwanda", *Social Justice Research* 24, pp. 85–106.

Le Blanc, S. A. (2003). *Constant battles: The myth of the peaceful, noble savage*. New York, NY: St. Martin's Press.

Liebmann, M. (2004). "Restorative justice and the prison system: A view from the UK". *VOMA Connections*, 17(Summer), 3–4.

Maguire, M. Morgan, M & R. Reiner (2007). *The Oxford Handbook of Criminology*, 4th Edition, Oxford: Oxford University Press.

Mander, H. (2004) *Cry, My Beloved Country: Reflections on the Gujarat Carnage*, New Delhi: Rainbow Publications.

Marshall, T. (1999). *Restorative Justice: An Overview*. Home Office. Research Development and Statistics Directorate. London, UK.

Marshall, T. and Merry, S. (1990) *Crime and Accountability: Victim-Offender Mediation in Practice*, London: HMSO.

Mattaini, M. and J. Strickland. (2006) Challenging collective violence: A scientific strategy, *International Journal of Psychology*, 41 (6), 500–513.

McCold, P. (1999). "A Reply to Walgrave", in P. McCold (ed) *The 4th International Conference on Restorative Justice for Juveniles*, Leuven, Belgium.

McNeese, C. A., and Thyer, B. A. (2004). Evidence-based practice and social work. *Journal of Evidence-Based Social Work*, 1(1), 7-25.

Miles, M. and Huberman, M. (1994). *Qualitative Data Analysis*. London: Sage.

Mill, J.S (1993). *Utilitarianism*, London: Everyman.

Montiel, C.J. and M. Wessells (2001). "Democratisation, Psychology and the Construction of cultures of Peace". *Journal of Peace Psychology*, 7, . pp 119-129.

Morrell, G., Scott, S., McNeish, D and S. Webster (2011). *The August Riots in England*, London: NatCen.

Morrison, B. (2003) . Regulating safe school communities: being responsive and restorative. *Journal of Educational Administration*. 41(6): 689-704.

Morrison, B. (2006) . Restorative Justice and Civil Society: Emerging Practice, Theory and Evidence. *Journal of Social Issues* (special issue 62(2)).2006

Olzak, S. (1992). *The Dynamics of Ethnic Competition and Conflict*. Stanford, CA: Stanford University Press.

Park, A. (2010). Community-based restorative transitional justice in Sierra Leone, *Contemporary Justice Review* Vol. 13, No. 1, pp. 95–119.

Pelikan, C. (2012). "Restorative justice in cases of partnership violence in Austria" in Gavrielides, T. (eds). *Rights and Restoration Within Youth Justice*, Whitby, ON: de Sitter Publications.

Prison Reform Working Group (2009). 'Locked up potential: a strategy for reforming prisons and rehabilitating prisoners', The Centre for Social Justice.

PUCL (2002). *Violence in Vadodara: A Report*. Vadodara: PUCL.

Roper, S.D and L.A. Barria (2009). "Why Do States Commission the Truth? Political

Considerations in the Establishment of African Truth and Reconciliation Commissions, *Hum Rights Review* 10, pp. 373–391.

Porter, E. (2007) *Peacebuilding: Women in International Perspective*, New York: Routlege.

Powers, J. (2008). "Restoring Harmony to Gujarat: Peace building after the 2002 riots", *Journal of the Third World Studies*, 103-115.

Riots, Communities and Victims Panel (2012). *After the Riots: The Final Report*, London.

Riots, Communities and Victims Panel (2011). *5 Days in August: An Interim Report on the 2011 English Riots*, London.

Rosenberg, M. L., O'Carroll, P. W. and Powell, K. E. (1992). "Let's Be Clear: Violence Is a Public Health Problem." *Journal of the American Medical Association* 267(22):3071072.

Shapland, J. et al. (2008). *Does restorative justice affect reconviction? The fourth report from the evaluation of three schemes* (Ministry of Justice Research Series 10/08). London: Ministry of Justice.

Shankar, J. and L. Gerstein (2007). "The Hindu-Muslim Conflict: A Pilot Study of Peacebuilding in Gujarat, India", *Journal of Peace Psychology*, 13(3), pp. 365-379.

Sharpe, S. (1998). *Restorative justice: A vision for healing and change*, Edmonton, Alberta, Canada: Mediation and Restorative Justice Centre.

Sherif, M. (1966). *In Common Predicament: Social Psychology of Intergroup Conflict and Cooperation*, Boston: Houghton Mifflin.

Sherman, L. and Strang, H. (2007) *Restorative justice: the evidence*. London: The Smith Institute.

Sherman, L., et al. (2000) *Recidivism Patterns in the Canberra Reintegrative Shaming Experiments (RISE)*, Canberra: Centre for Restorative Justice.

Simons, H. (1980). *Towards a science of the singular: Essays about case study in educational research and evaluation*. Norwich, UK: University of East Anglia, Centre for Applied Research in Education

Smillie, I. and J. Hailey. (2001). *Managing for Change: Leadership, Strategy and Management in Asian NGOs*, London: Earthscan.

Stake, R. E. (1995). The art of case study research. Thousand Oaks, CA: Sage.

Tajfel, H. and J.C Turner (1986). "An Integrated Theory of Social Conflict". In S. Worchel and W. Austin (Eds), *Psychology of Intergroup Relations*. Chicago: Nelson Hall, pp. 7-24.

Thayer, B. A. (2004). *Darwin and international relations: On the evolutionary origins of war and ethnic conflict*. Lexington, Kentucky: The University of Kentucky Press.

Tilly, C. (1978). *From Mobilisation to Revolution*. Reading, MA: Addison-Wesley.

Tilly, C. et al (1975). *The Rebellious Century*, Cambridge, MA: Harvard University Press.

Valiñas M. and K. Vanspauwen (2009). "Truth-seeking after violent conflict: experiences from South Africa and Bosnia and Herzegovina", *Contemporary Justice Review* Vol. 12, No. 3, pp. 269–288.

Vancouver Association for Restorative Justice (unpublished, August 2011). From *Glowing Hearts to Burning Cars to Restored Community*, Vancouver: VARJ. http://www.iars.org.uk/sites/default/files/VARJ%20submission%20to%20 Vancouver%20Riot%20Review%20of%202011.pdf

Varadarajan, S. (2002). *Gujarat: The making of a Tragedy*. New Delhi: Penguin.

Victim Support (2010). *Victims' Justice: What victims and witness really want from sentencing*, London: Victim Support.

Walgrave, L. (2012). "Restorative justice and human rights in a democratic society", in Gavrielides, T. (eds). *Rights and Restoration Within Youth Justice*, Whitby, ON: de Sitter Publications.

Whyte, B. (2009) *Youth Justice in Practice*, Bristol: Policy Press.

World Health Organisation. (2002) *World Report on Violence and Health*. Geneva: WHO.

Yin, R. K. (1984). *Case study research: Design and methods*. Newbury Park, CA: Sage.

Zehr, H. (1990) *Changing Lenses: A New Focus for Crime and Justice*, Scottdale, Pennsylvania Waterloo, Ontario: Herald Press.

Appendix A: **About IARS**

IARS is a leading, international think-tank with a charitable **mission to give everyone a chance to forge a safer, fairer and more inclusive society.** IARS achieves its charitable aims by producing **evidence-based** solutions to **current** social problems, sharing best practice and by supporting **young people** to shape decision making. IARS is an international expert in **restorative justice, human rights** and **inclusion, citizenship** and **user-led research.**

IARS is known for its robust, independent, evidence-based approach to solving current social problems, and we are considered a pioneer in user-involvement and the application of user-led research methods. IARS delivers its charitable mission:

- **By** carrying out action research that is independent, credible, focused and current
- **By** acting as a network that brings people and ideas together, communicates best practice and encourages debates on current social policy matters
- **By** supporting the individual (with an emphasis on young people) to carry out their own initiatives to shape decision-making
- **By** being an authoritative, independent and evidence-based voice on current social policy matters.

As an independent, advocacy organisation we have a mission to **transform young people's lives** by enabling them to have a better future, and participate equally and democratically in civic life. IARS young people learn to inform policies and practices affecting them whether at a local, regional, national or international level. IARS membership is open to anyone who believes in the charity's mission. Membership benefits package:

- 25% discount to our **Annual Conference**
- 1 hard copy per annum of *Youth Voice Journal*
- Free membership to the **Restorative Justice Research Network**
- 25% discount to all our **hard copy books and publications** including *Youth Voice Journal*
- 1 hard copy of our **annual impact report**
- 25% discount of advertising space on our hard and soft copy publications.

To become a member:
Email: **contact@iars.org.uk** Tel: **+44(0) 20 7820 0945 www.iars.org.uk**

Appendix B: **Centre for Restorative Justice**

The Centre for Restorative Justice is an initiative by the Simon Fraser University School of Criminology. The Centre for Restorative Justice, in partnership with individuals, the community, justice agencies and the University, exists to support and promote the principles and practices of restorative justice. The Centre provides education, innovative program models, training, evaluation and research through a resource centre and meeting place that facilitates outreach, promotion, dialogue and advocacy.

The Centre is directed by Professor Brenda Morrison. In consultation and partnership with community and government agencies, the Centre for Restorative Justice provides a number of services and initiatives such as research on RJ programmes and practices, programme development and evaluation services and development of Aboriginal programmes involving directly recruited Aboriginal graduate students in special cohort programmes.

www.sfu.ca/crj

Appendix B: **About the Restorative Justice Research Network (RJRN)**

The RJRN sits within IARS and is an **international, non-profit, research community** that was set up to:

- disseminate cutting edge research on restorative justice
- connect researchers, policy-makers and practitioners in restorative justice worldwide
- create networking and collaboration opportunities within the international restorative justice movement
- identify best practices internationally, evaluate, promote and publish them
- push the barriers of restorative justice and create new knowledge.
  The network is headed by IARS Director Dr. Theo Gavrielides.

RJRN Membership
RJRN has a large membership of individuals and organisations from around the world.

To join email **RestorativeJustice@iars.org.uk** or visit
http://www.iars.org.uk/content/RJRN

RJRN Projects & Services
The RJRN is running a number of international programmes and services that are available to all its members. To find out how to get involved and to ask for more information email RestorativeJustice@iars.org.uk . These programmes are:

- **The International Symposia on Restorative Justice & Human Rights**
- **Regular e-newsletters** including updates on key policy and research news internationally
- **E-publications** including papers in leading peer review journals
- **The seminars** "Drawing together research, policy and practice for restorative justice"
- **Various desk publications** such as *Restorative Justice Theory & Practice: Addressing the Discrepancy, Rights & Restoration within Youth Justice*, and *Restorative Justice and the Secure Estate: Alternatives for Young People What is Restorative Justice?*

"Restorative Justice is an **ethos** with practical goals, among which is **to restore harm** by including affected parties in a (direct or indirect) **encounter** and a process of understanding through voluntary and honest dialogue. Restorative justice adopts a fresh approach to conflicts and their control, retaining at the same time certain rehabilitative goals" (Gavrielides 2007: 139)

Appendix D: **About the author**

D r. Theo Gavrielides is the **Founder and Director** of Independent Academic Research Studies (IARS). He is also a **Visiting Professor in Youth Policy** at Buckinghamshire New University, a **Visiting Professorial Research Fellow** at Panteion University of Social & Political Science (Greece), a **Visiting Senior Research Fellow** at the International Centre for Comparative Criminological Research (ICCCR) at Open University (UK) and a Visiting Scholar at the Centre for Criminology and Justice Research Department of Justice Mount Royal University (Canada).

Professor Gavrielides is also a **Trustee** of the Anne Frank Trust , an **Advisory Board Member** of the Institute for Diversity Research, Inclusivity, Communities and Society (IDRICS), Buckinghamshire New University, and a **Member** of the Scrutiny and Involvement Panel of the Crown Prosecution Service (London).

Dr. Gavrielides obtained a **Doctorate in Law** from the London School of Economics and Political Science (PhD, 2005) and a **Masters in Human Rights Law** from Nottingham University (LL.M in Human Rights Law, 2000). He **graduated from the Faculty of Laws** of the National University of Athens and practised law at Gavrielides & Co.

Dr. Gavrielides has published extensively in academic journals. His 2007 book *"Restorative Justice Theory and Practice"* was published by the European Institute for Crime Prevention and Control affiliated with the United Nations (HEUNI) and Criminal Justice Press. His 2012 book *"Rights and Restoration within Youth Justice"* was published by de Sitter Publications.

A list of Gavrielides' publications can be found at:
www.iars.org.uk/ iarsusers/theo-gavrielides